"Not only is Bob a trustful and highly professional expert, *̶* engaging speaker, Bob is also one of the nicest men I have ev̶ wisdom of experience with astounding vigour and charisma. I highly recommend him." **Elizabeth Grimaud**, AFCP (French Speakers Association)

"I watched Bob Hooey deliver a speech in Cape Town, SA when he was feeling far less than 100%. The audience never knew. That's what a pro does. Shows up and delivers!" **Shep Hyken**, CSP, CPAE, Past President NSA, professional speaker and customer service expert

**"Bob 'Idea Man' Hooey** is a Master of Public speaking, not only in Canada, but internationally. Not only has he motivated, inspired, and energized tens of thousands of people in his audiences worldwide, he also takes the time to work with aspiring and developing speakers to help them hone their skills and perfect their craft, so they can be their very best on the platform and in the business. If you are interested in public speaking, or you are developing a career as a professional speaker, trainer, or keynoter, Bob's wisdom will help you get there." **Sarah Elaine Eaton**, Ph.D.

"We were thrilled when we secured Bob Hooey to speak at our annual convention in April (2015). Having heard so much about him over the years, I found him true to his reputation - **an absolute professional**, keeping the client in contact and informed, sending through requirements early and confirming all that we needed from him. And then on the day, delivering a wonderful, fun and engaging presentation that both communicated Bob's message and fit in with our theme brilliantly. I would love to work with Bob again." **Charlotte Kemp**, Convention Chair PSA SA 2015 Convention in Cape Town, SA

"If your company needs new and creative ideas, I highly recommend Canada's Ideaman, Bob Hooey. He has sincere passion for helping others to succeed and guiding them to reach their highest potential. You are leaving a legacy. Thank you." **Debra Kasowski**, Author of GPS Your Best Life

"Good news is always good! Congratulations on this wonderful achievement (Spirit of CAPS) - well deserved, I'm sure! And how gracious of you to "share" this award with so many others - you're a true leader and a real gentleman!" **Chris Ford**, DTM, Past International President (2007-2008) Toastmasters International

"Congratulations on winning the Spirit of CAPS award. I can think of no one who more richly deserved the award. Your acceptance speech moved us all reminding us of what's it's all about. Your humility and graciousness were inspiring. Congratulations again my friend." **Michael Bayer**, CSP, 2012 President CAPS Winnipeg

*"Bob 'Idea Man' Hooey is a mentor to many and has done great things for CAPS Edmonton. Bob has also provided me with innovative ideas to help grow my business. His commitment to CAPS, the speaking profession, and professional speakers is admirable! It is a pleasure to recommend Bob."* **Charmaine Hammond**, Hammond International

***"Bob 'Idea Man' Hooey*** *is an exceptional speaker and facilitator who helps businesses and organizations grow profit and create effective teams. This leadership and sales expert has written nearly a dozen books, travels the globe speaking to managers, corporations, and non-profits, increasing morale as well as profits. Bob is a leader within the speaking industry and is beloved by his peers for his mentorship, warmth and high skill. I highly recommend Bob as a speaker. He'll be the one your employees and conference attendees talk about."* **Shawne Duperon**, CEO, ShawneTV (3-time Emmy award winner)

*"I had the pleasure of hearing and watching Bob Hooey deliver a keynote speech several years ago when he gave a presentation at a Toastmasters International Convention. Bob impressed me greatly with his professionalism, energy, and ability to connect with his audience while giving them value. I heartily recommend this talented speaker and "Idea Farmer" to all who want to move to the next level."* **Dilip Abayasekara**, DTM, AS

*"Bob has coached the Senior Executive members of the District 42 Toastmasters for several years, serving as a Trainer & Mentor at our annual experiential training event. In addition to sharing his knowledge and experience with the leaders in our organization, he has been very helpful & influential to me personally. Bob is worth every penny of your investment in his services... and then some! But let's not tell him that!!"* **Troy Wruck**, DTM, Past District 42 Governor, Toastmasters International

*"We were delighted when Bob 'Idea Man' Hooey agreed to speak at our Professional Speaking Association October event in Scotland. Bob was an absolute pleasure to deal with – professional and organised he provided the information we required in good time and kept in touch in the lead up to the event to ensure everything ran smoothly. On the night, he shared valuable tips and ideas with our members to help them to grow their speaking business. He also demonstrated further professionalism and expertise when he stepped in at the last minute to speak for a for a further 20 minutes when our schedule changed unexpectedly, and for that I am very grateful – thanks Bob!"* **Mel Sherwood**, 2016-2017 President, PSA-Scotland

*"Thanks, Bob, for your enthusiastic and ongoing support of The Business Link as a learning session speaker. And congratulations on your "Spirit of CAPS" award at the Canadian Association of Professional Speakers annual convention in Toronto. Well deserved!!"* **Cathy Goulet**, Manager, The Business Link

# PREPARE YOURSELF TO WIN!

## IDEA-RICH SUCCESS SECRETS

**BOB 'IDEA MAN' HOOEY**

AUTHOR, LEGACY OF LEADERSHIP

3rd Edition – updated and expanded

*Destiny is not a matter of chance, it is a matter of choice; it is not a thing to be waited for, it is a thing to be achieved.*
William Jennings Bryan

*Dedicated to those top-level individuals and leaders who are committed to winning in their lives and those of their teams, and who are willing to prepare for that goal.*

**Success Publications**

www.SuccessPublications.ca
Box 10, Egremont, AB T0A 0Z0

# Prepare yourself to WIN!

*"I hated every minute of training, but I said, don't quit. Suffer now and live the rest of your life as a champion."* **Muhammad Ali**

Building a successful leadership or sales career or a profitable business takes hard work and applied energy. If it was that easy, everyone would be doing it. Sometimes you will reach the end of your strength or run head-on into a roadblock or wall – stay the course and continue. Prepare for that challenge! Prepare yourself to WIN!

### You **can live the rest of your life as a champion.**
- A champion of your **creativity**.
- A champion of your **courage**.
- A champion of your **causes** and concerns.
- A champion of your sales team and your **clients**.
- A champion of living and sharing your **message**.
- A champion of your successful **career** path.
- A champion of your **dreams** (turning them into reality).

*This is something experienced first-hand. I worked to overcome serious challenges and difficulties to prepare for the first level audition, while working towards the Toastmasters International's professional level Accredited Speaker designation. There were times I thought about throwing in the towel. When I spoke in San Diego (1995) and was not successful, I pulled myself up and worked harder for my opportunity to speak the following year in Saint Louis (1996).*

*When I again fell short, I was tempted to quit. I was frustrated, disappointed in my performance, and inclined to move on; to forget my dream of becoming a professional speaker. But something would not let me quit! My success team would not let me quit either. They believed even when my belief wavered.*

*In 1998, when I finally walked across a Palm Desert, California stage to become the 48th person in the world to earn this coveted professional level Toastmasters International designation, I felt like a champion who had gone 15 rounds and emerged bloodied, but unbeaten. The applause and cheers of 2200 fellow Toastmasters still echo in my ears, and my heart. It was a pinnacle point in my life as a professional speaker; the first of many.*
**If you would like to see it** follow this link: www.ideaman.net/SoC.htm

*Was it the three speeches I prepared and presented on the Toastmasters world stage that earned this coveted professional designation? Partially! Looking back, I believe it was the hundreds of prepared presentations given in various Toastmaster clubs and in community events across the country, as well as for paying clients that built the foundations for this eventual success on the world stage.*

*I've faced challenges in other areas of my life (business, financial, physical, and relationships) where I applied some of the same preparation, determination, discipline, and asking for help to move through to the winner's zone. Moving into the winner's zone means moving out of your comfort zone.*

**You can succeed in whatever field you enter if you are willing to prepare. You can become a top performing professional; be the champion you were meant to be. If I can do it, so can you!**

The **Indiana University Hoosiers** basketball team were proven winners. They remained undefeated throughout their 1976 season and captured the NCAA National Championship under coach Bobby Knight. The '60 Minutes' commentator asked him about this amazing feat and why they were so successful. He asked, *"Was it their will to succeed?"*
*"The will to succeed is important,"* replied Knight, *"but I'll tell you what is more important –* **it's the will to prepare**. *It's the will to go out there every day, training and building those muscles and sharpening those skills."*

- Want to be a champion salesperson? – **Prepare**
- Want to be an effective leader? – **Prepare**
- Want to create a profitable and winning business? – **Prepare**
- Want to be a powerful presenter or speaker? – **Prepare**
- Want to live an effective and meaningful life? – **Prepare**

**Bill Bradley** (scholar, basketball star, and former US Senator) reminds us, *"When you are not practicing, remember someone somewhere is practicing; and when you meet him or her, they will win."* Prepare, practice, and act decisively when the time is right! Prepare and make this your time to win!

**"You were meant to WIN, but to be a winner, you must plan to win, prepare to win, and expect to win!"** Zig Ziglar

# A note as we begin our journey to your success…

Winning isn't everything, but the willingness to prepare and proceed is!

**A fundamental question?** What do you mean or visualize when you see yourself winning?

- Is it a business or leadership career success?
- Is it a sport related or physical achievement?
- Is it a personal relationship or family success?
- Is it another personal goal or dream?

It is important to visualize where you are going and to define as specifically and clearly as possible where you want to end up. This helps you prepare and make whatever changes in your life and business to enable you to move confidently ahead in this goal.

**Definition of *winner*** – Webster's Dictionary
**One that wins**: such as:

- one that is successful through praiseworthy ability and hard work.
- a victor especially in games and sports
- one that wins admiration.

**But how do you define it for yourself?**

For example, if your goal is to run a marathon and you diligently prepare and tone your body, is winning being the first person to cross the finish line, or is it for you to simply cross the finish line or to achieve a personal best time? Makes a difference in how you see yourself succeed and how you prepare for that goal.

We'll cover elements that will benefit you in whatever winning goal you have in mind. We'll include tips and techniques in these areas along with some general ones for you to ponder and apply. We've put them into easily accessed sections, so you can go right to the ones you need now.

- **Creativity and mental skills**
- **Leadership skills (personal and positional)**
- **Personal and professional productivity skills**
- **Communication skills**
- **Sales and customer service skills**
- **Motivation and encouragement**

We've drawn from our Idea-rich business and leadership success series in creating this blended success manual.

Visit: **www.SuccessPublications.ca** to order the full set for your success resource library.

Wishing you outstanding success as you prepare to amaze yourself in reaching and surpassing your goals.

I believe you have the power inside you to make your dreams a reality – you must prepare to access it and apply it... to win!

**Bob 'Idea Man' Hooey**
Fellow traveller and guide
www.ideaman.net
www.BobHooey.training

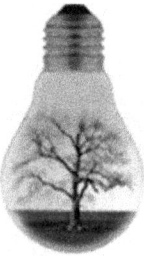

*"In an era when companies see online support to shield themselves from 'costly' interactions with their customers, it's time to consider an entirely different approach: building human-centric customer (client) service through great people and clever technology. So, get to know your customers. Humanize them. Humanize yourself. It's worth it."*
**Kristin Smaby, 'Being Human is Good Business'**

**PRO-TIP:** It has been said the "largest room in the world is room for improvement". Within these pages you can glean the tools to improve your personal life and professional career. Your communication skills will be enhanced as you speak with clarity and simplicity, all the while using an economy of high impact words that will penetrate the heart of the listener. At a glance you will be able to analyse your audience and project a message to ears that will hear and understand.
© **Wayne Land**, Oakwood Management Ltd. *(Editor's note: Wayne and Bob went to high school together and reconnected a few years back.)*

8

# Table of Contents

**PRO-TIP:** Remember relationships underpin everything we do. Take time to 'Be There' and genuinely listen when you are in conversation with your people. Look them in the eye and listen as if it's the best conversation you've ever had.
© *Lindsay Adams*, *CSP* www.therelationshipsguy.com.au

# Getting started

**Welcome fellow ladies and gentlemen in leadership!** Welcome to the *never-ending* journey of an evolving career and management focus on personal leadership development and coaching. A competitive change in global perspective has placed a new focus and pressure on finding and applying more productive uses of your assets and updating your team members' skills to grow on site and compete successfully.

Taking personal leadership in your own career growth and success is worth the investment. This is where you apply *leverage* to dynamically succeed! Too many leaders are *blind* to the opportunities and responsibilities of creating and nurturing those who would follow them. Too many, miss the opportunity (are blind) to play an active part in the selection, growth, and success of those who would succeed them; those who would help them succeed as leaders.

*"Avoid being the blind leading the blind ... leave behind a 'Legacy of Leadership'."* **Bob 'Idea Man' Hooey**

Leadership can be a *lonely* and *frustrating* road to walk. There will be times when you wonder if it is *worth the effort* you give. I know I have! **'Prepare Yourself to WIN!** is my contribution to helping you work through the frustrations, challenges, and lessons; to see your efforts bear positive fruit. This book was written to share proven tips and idea-rich techniques we felt would be helpful in your quest for leadership and significance.

Recently, workplace coaching has taken on a new, more effective focus. Leading edge employees, managers, and successful executives have experienced positive results in enlisting a leadership coach to help them improve in specific areas or to achieve specific goals. **Striving for significance leads along this path.**

*People have been going outside the corporate arena and enlisting or recruiting personal or leadership coaches. They want to change, to improve their performance, and to enhance their ability to win! Strive for significance - lead on purpose!*

Many world leaders, executives, and innovative managers have also seen the wisdom and a positive return on their investment of time and resources in training and **coaching their employees and future leaders for optimal results**.

Things are changing in the boardrooms, factories, and on the sales floors of businesses across North America and the globe. **Are you?**

Leaders are changing as well, with more women taking on important leadership roles and proving themselves worthy as they inspire other women to follow their lead. Bravo!

**People generally experience problems and challenges in their performance for four major reasons:**

- **Poor or inadequate training**
- **Inadequate equipment or support services**
- **Time constraints and poor time management**
- **Motivation**

Unfortunately, many of these reasons can be traced back to poor or *uninspired* leadership. We've included tips for each of these areas.

Many 21st Century leaders are moving into the coaching role as an effective style and skill in helping their teams grow and succeed.

- **Leadership coaching**, in its essence, will help you discover the area(s) which are acting as roadblocks for the person being coached.
- **Leadership coaching** can help you turn roadblocks into stepping-stones for increased success, productivity, and a real sense of satisfaction on the job.
- **Leadership coaching** can bring you a sense of satisfaction as the coach, too – bringing out the best and in seeing your people productively grow and win!

One of the most important aspects of your leadership growth and continued success is measured by the investment in your team and the results of those efforts. Keep this mantra in mind!

### *"You win, when your people win!"* **Bob 'Idea Man' Hooey**

*I had the opportunity to repeatedly drive this idea-rich strategy home a few years back when I was engaged to work with the President and senior management team for one of Canada's 50 Best Managed Companies, The Brick.*

*Over a period of four months, we explored ways of helping these men and women hone their leadership skills to better lead their respective teams. The results were astounding!*

*The following year they broke the billion-dollar retail sales mark for the first time in their 33-year history.*

This is a lesson learned from working with and studying the actions of North America's leaders in various industries, including the volunteer sector. This, coupled with my own experience in a variety of leadership roles, has reinforced my contention that **"You win, when your team wins!"**

**'Prepare Yourself to WIN!'** was originally published twice as an e-book. We decided to update it and expand this year. I've learned a few more lessons and tips in my own leadership journey. ☺

I trust you will find solid value in what is shared here and create a **legacy of leadership and significance.**

**Bob 'Idea Man' Hooey**
**A *'serious'* leader in progress**

*"I hear, and I forget.*

*I see, and I remember.*

*I do, and I understand!"*

## Confucius

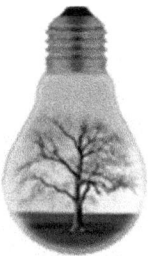

Your future leans heavily on what I call the **3P's of business success. Your active leadership makes this happen.**

**Positioning:** Constant effort on your part to ensure you are positioned in the minds of your clients, with the products and services they need, before they need them! A success foundation!

**Promoting:** Constant effort to ensure they know who you are, what you can do for them and where you are located. Business basics 101!

**Performing:** Constant effort, by every member of your team. Ensure that each client contact is a positive one that reinforces your commitment to serve them, now and in the future. Customer Service!

# How to get the 'best' from 'Prepare Yourself to WIN!'

'**Prepare Yourself to WIN!** – *Idea-rich success secrets* contains a range of tips, techniques, and ideas to help you improve the way you 'train' and lead your team for shared growth and profitable long-term success with your clients. It evolved into its present format (from a college level program) with the inclusion of stories, ideas, and first-hand experience based on conversations, copious notes, and first-hand observations of productive fellow leaders, sales professionals, and successful retailers. It was made personal from my own experiences leading and being on a variety of teams across North America and the globe. It is seasoned with my own leadership, sales, and customer service tips as well as experiences in retail, direct sales, and professional services.

It has been updated with a focus to assist professionals, owners, and leaders like you; to more profitably enhance their business with enhanced innovative strategies. It is designed to guide those who want to take personal leadership over their own lives and actions; providing a purpose and making a positive contribution in the lives of their teams and client interactions.

**This is not just a book for casual reading.** It is a book to be *chewed*, to be dipped into, and leveraged as a resource or reference guide. It is a workbook with provocative questions that help you decide what you want to accomplish with your life, your leadership, and with your client and team relationships. It is your resource, so mark it, highlight it, and make notes in the margins.

**To get the best from this book**, first visit the Table of Contents to identify which sections, chapters, and/or topics meet your most critical, time sensitive needs. Read them carefully and make sure you understand the guidelines and advice given. Some of the topics may not be of direct interest to you (now) depending on your needs. You may wish to read some of the other chapters so that you can understand the needs of other leaders' scenarios.

**'Prepare Yourself to WIN!' does not contain ALL the answers.** It contains a collection of thoughts, notes, clippings, tips, techniques, lessons learned, and ideas shared primarily from one learner, one business leader's (one retailer's) viewpoint, mine. It is simply intended as an aid to your reflection, learning, and inspiration – a resource that you can draw upon. Its aim is to give you a creative resource that, when applied and practiced with your teams, will help you develop and build both your confidence and profitable competence as a leader, manager, and business owner.

A more productive approach would be to take the tips and concepts presented here and blend them with your own leadership style, personality, and creativity. Keep in mind your own time constraints and 'comfort zone' as a leader, manager, or professional. Generate unique and perhaps personalized ideas on how you can create, give, and improve your interaction and action with your teams and clients. **'Prepare Yourself to WIN! – 3rd edition'** is designed to offer you flexibility in how you leverage it for your personal and professional use.

1) You can easily sit down for an hour or two and read it **cover-to-cover**. This is a great way to start by getting a feel for what is included, especially for newer or emerging leaders, managers, or owners (those who want to take more personal leadership for their lives and better equip their teams to grow) who want to gain the full benefit from their investment.

**A word of advice: 'Prepare Yourself to WIN!'** is the result of 29 plus years of personal study, first-hand experience, and observation in a variety of leadership, retail, business, and sales roles; additionally, coaching as well as support for executive clients and their respective teams. It might seem overwhelming or confusing at first with the range of information included here. Once you have done a quick read of the whole book, identify sections or tips that interest you and work on manageable chunks.

2) You can select one chapter or section and work to incorporate the ideas you discover into your own specific leadership role, client engagement, or business situation.

3) You can look at the Table of Contents and jump straight to the tips or areas of study that particularly interest you.

We have attempted to incorporate something of benefit for everyone, regardless of your current level or skill in business. You might even find some *seemingly contradictory* advice in different parts of the book! ☺ This is because there is no single, universal 'right answer' – you must find what is a right fit for you, your objective, and your team's specific needs.

**What works for you is what is best.** Choose it, try it, and adapt it as needed to serve you in your quest to be a more effective businessperson and impactful leader. Take control of how you allocate, invest, or leverage your time and interaction with your staff and clients. We've written it to help you guide your teams to become more productive and profitably enhance your team skills and business dealings with your clients.

# Creativity and mental skills

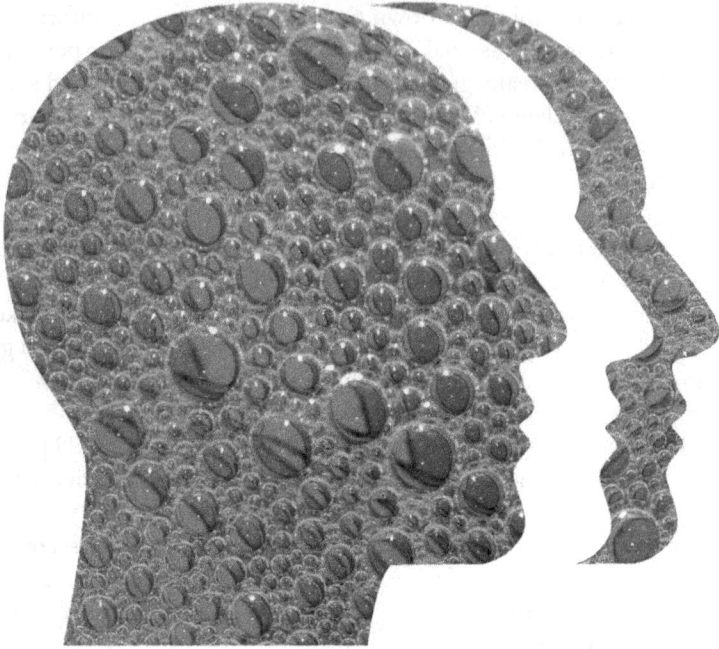

## Change is a creative choice.

In life, we have the opportunity thrust upon us to make changes. A death, a major illness, **or a major economic upheaval** can force us to take stock of our lives at that point, and perhaps force some radical changes. In our changing economy, we find businesses and government agencies being stretched and tested. Staffing has become more challenging, so has training and marketing. Customers are becoming more demanding and specific in what they want.

Change is pushed on us everywhere we turn. **We can't avoid change, can we?** That's what too many business owners think and miss their full potential. Isn't it better to seize the opportunities to change and grow? Isn't it better to remain open to learn, stretch, and to push yourself past your comfort zone?

**This change is a creative choice! Life is a series of changes and choices; why not control their direction and pace?**

*"Searching for the peak performer within yourself has one basic meaning - You recognize yourself as a person who was born, not as a peak performer but as a learner. With the capacity to grow, change, and reach for the highest possibilities of human nature, you regard yourself as a person in process. Not perfect, but a person who keeps asking: What more can I be? What else can I achieve that will benefit my organization and myself?"*
**Charles Garfield**

**Ask yourself a few questions.** Allow your honest reactions to reflect the changes in your attitudes and actions that may need to be addressed to maximize your life and dealings in relation to your role at work.

What do I really want my life to accomplish?
What is my biggest dream?
What would I like my team, company, or organization to accomplish?
Where do I want my career to go?
What am I afraid of?
What is stopping me?
What keeps me up at night?
What do I need to change to make it work?
When do I need to change it?
When will I commit to start making these changes?

**Will you have the courage to change?** Will you commit to be your best and to creatively build your organization to maximize its potential?

 Remember the words of retailer J.C. Penney: ***"No one need live a minute longer as he/she is, because the creator endowed us with the ability to change ourselves."***

Answering these questions will have given you a glimpse of what needs to be changed to make your dreams and goals a reality. The secret is in putting foundations under your dreams and actions under your goals.

The secret to **unlocking your 'creativity' potential** is in accessing your ability to embrace and utilize change for mutual benefit. **The choice is yours!**

 ***"Think left and think right and think low and think high. Oh, the thinks you can think up if only you try."***
**Dr. Seuss**

# Food for thought... Feeding your creative process

Leverage these tips to help you feed your mind and fuel the creative process in your day-to-day role on the job. Use these as warm ups, or tune-ups to keep your mind fresh, alert, and alive.

*"Great minds discuss ideas. Average minds discuss events. Small minds discuss people."* **Henry Thomas Buckle**

**Warm up your creativity** - take two unrelated objects; Imagine comparisons or connections between them. For example, a diamond and an elephant. Both have different facets and come from Africa.

**Practice mental pinball** - Take one word or thought; See if you can freely associate 10 - 20 items or thoughts.

**Look at other areas**, worlds or industries to spark the solution you need – e.g. frequent flyer miles and coffee cards.

**Creative environment** – for example: casual clothes, warm room, soft couch, fireplace, soft music, walking outdoors on a lovely day, or working in a dimly lit room.

**What would a famous person do?** The Pope, Jay Leno, JFK, Mother Theresa, or… *(pick someone you admire for their creative abilities)*

**Think 'POSITIVE'** – i.e. let's look at the *'workable'* parts.

**Go for quantity if you want quality**. Ideas beget more ideas! Pick the best ones from the bunch and save the remainder for another look.

**Play to keep your creativity alive** *(remember your child)*, explore and have fun with the challenge.

Solutions come when you least expect them - **relax!**

**Team works** - apply the power of collective thinking! Create a success team, master mind group, or un-official team of advisors!

Information, time, and the ability to solve problems creatively are the most valued currencies in business.

**Learn to use technology**, attend a seminar, listen to an MP3, read a book, buy some re-active thinking software.

**Being '*wrong*' is part of the creative process**. To reach success, increase your failure rate; but don't fail to learn the lesson from the lesson!

**Get past the fear** of looking stupid.

**Believe in 'YOU'** as a creative source. Belief proceeds creation!

**Don't let the negativity get to you.**

**Tackle your fears** to unleash your creativity.

## A few thoughts to feed your creativity muscles.

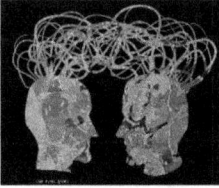

**Mental exercise** is a daily regimen and is just as important to your life as regular exercise and a healthy diet. You need to feed and exercise your mind if you want to be creative and discover the innovative solutions to your customer's needs.

These tips will give your mind what it needs to get into shape and keep into shape for creative application on the job and in your life in general.

**PRO-TIP:** A technique from my advertising world is to **thumbnail ideas** – generate ideas (in a small mock up drawing) to get them down on paper. When a thumbnail of a print advertisement or a TV ad is created it may start with a visual image and then the written part or visa versa. For TV ads and videos, I would write notes on the thumbnail about the sound, voice (if there is one), action, and/or movement. The idea is to generate as many ideas, as quickly as possible – don't edit while generating the idea. Then go back to all the thumbnail sketches and determine which merit further development. The technique allows you to use both sides of the brain to quickly generate ideas. Don't worry about being a great artist to use this approach – it's simply about getting your ideas down quickly.
© *David Saxby* www.sparkcommunications.com

# Six Creative Indicators

Can you tell who is more likely to be a creative addition to your team? Can you separate the 'really' creative from the herd? Well, according to research, there are six basic indicators that might help in your quest to attract creative people for your team. People who rank high or exhibit more of these characteristics tend to be more creative.

## Idea volume and fluency

This is an area where volume 'actually' counts. It may take 30 average ideas to yield one great one. Creative people tend to be better at generating ideas, even if most of them have little long term or applicable commercial value. Our minds are very much like a 'muscle' in that we tend to work better when we warm them up. They work better when they are exercised on a regular basis, too. Our best ideas often come after we work through the more basic ones.

## Slow to jump to conclusions or judge

You tend to get more high-quality ideas when judgment is withheld. This is the secret to effective brainstorming or 'Thunder-thinking'. Judging cuts off the creative flow of ideas. Judging tends to look for what doesn't fit or won't work versus exploring possibilities and potential. Creativity is willing to explore the options and potentials.

## Imagination and flexibility

Creativity in its essence is based on flexible thinking. Creative people tend to exhibit almost a kid-like curiosity about life. Acting as if the world can be as you imagine it enhances your creativity. *"The best way to predict the future is to create or invent it."*

## Concentration and focus

Both these traits are 'critical aspects' of creativity. Concentration is staying focused on a subject, even when you are tired, bored, or frustrated. Creative behaviors ignore or tune out distractions and outside stimuli while working to solve a problem or reach a goal.

## Able to deal with ambiguity

Creativity is dealing with the vague and unformed to create the clear and concise. Creative people tend to be able to handle ambiguity where there is no clearly defined right or wrong. Creative people have a willingness to see all sides of a situation and to remain in questioning mode rather than rushing to find the answer. They keep going past the 'first' right answer to explore for the 'best' answer or innovative solution.

## Able to handle disorder

Creative people tend to handle or even prefer disorder. Forget the stereotype of the absent-minded professor with stacks all around the office. This may be valid, but **disorder is not necessarily 'mess'**. Disorder refers to non-linear thinking, shaking up the normal order, status quo, or non-symmetrical design.

Keep these six indicators in mind when you are looking to recruit a member of your Mastermind Alliance, leadership, sales and marketing team, or support team. People do exhibit their creative traits if you are willing to look and analyze their behaviour. Remember we can unleash our creativity, too.

## Ideas that are weird – perhaps?

Innovation and idea generation are basically about being curious and courageous; curious about life, courageous about challenging the status quo, and then making changes to make it better.

This is where those who lead creatively excel. They are not afraid to go outside the confines of their narrow field and to borrow, beg, and sometimes 'steal' ideas from other fields and industries. **Great ideas are transferable!** It is a good management practice to look at your 'norms' and ask yourself the 'contrarian' or flip side of the equation questions. This is where innovation and the real creative spark exist. That doesn't mean you always throw away what you are currently using. At times it is still very effective and may be the most productive use of your time, resources, and energy. **What if there is a better way, a more productive way, a more cost-effective way, and your competitor finds it first?** Hmm?

The secret to thriving in our competitive and, by now everyone understands, globally competitive market is being constantly on the 'improve' and sometimes that means 'improve' to find the answers to the questions your existing and potential clients are asking. So, keep questioning and keep on the quest to tap into your creative genius!

21

# So, you have a problem… that's great!

So, you have a problem, that's great! Are you crazy? …NO! Someone once told me that, **"I'd get paid or determine my value, by my ability to solve problems."** That sage advice has proven to be *very profitable* over the years! If it was easy, everyone would be doing it, and the competition would be intense. But, as many customers will tell you, most businesses are not in the problem-solving field. Your ability to solve your client's problems will be directly related to the number of sales and continued growth of your firm.

The more successfully and **creatively you and your staff solve these problems**, the more referrals and fans you'll see. The more that you personally are a solution-oriented owner, manager, or employee, the more dramatically your pay-check and career path will be affected.

I apply this **simple 4-stage process for dealing with problems or challenges.** This is an effective way to deal **creatively** with customer complaints and concerns as well as other areas of your business and life. These ideas work with leadership, creative, strategic planning, and normal problem solving.

Since so many of my clients and audiences have a need to be productive in dealing with customers, I write from that perspective. This section is excerpted from, **"Make ME Feel Special! - *Idea-rich customer service strategies*". Visit www.SuccessPublications.ca.**

Invest time in making sure you fully **UNDERSTAND** the problem.
The key to understanding is to **IDENTIFY** the real cause.
Take time to fully explore and **DISCUSS** all the possible solutions.
Act to **SOLVE** or fully resolve the problem.

"The secret to idea-rich, EFFECTIVE, business success" (dealing with their problems either in advance or as they occur) is to go through this process *with* your clients (engage them in the process). After the problem has been successfully resolved, invest in the relationship to **go the extra mile**.

By that, I mean, doing something *unexpected* to assist the client or to show them you appreciate the opportunity to prove your commitment to their well-being. This will help turn an angry or frustrated client into a fan, or better yet… a champion for you and your business.

**Stage One: Understanding the problem**: Often a problem is a perception of a difference of what we expected to happen and what happened. Here are 3 action steps to help:

**Gather ALL the facts**. Be thorough and investigate. Let the client talk!

**Listen carefully** and don't be defensive. Wait until they've finished talking and ask more questions to draw them out, to find out their REAL concerns.

**Rephrase** or repeat the problem back to the client to make sure you've heard it correctly and understand what needs to be resolved. Agree at this stage.

It's important at this stage to make sure you don't fall into the trap of denying or trying to avoid the problem. Or worse yet, blaming or attacking someone else, or demonstrating the same negative emotions in response to a customer's complaint.

Just listen and get the facts!

**Stage Two: Identify the Cause of the Problem**: You might ask yourself or your client a few questions to find out what may have caused the problem.

**What has happened**? Listen and ask questions. Get a true assessment of current situation.

**What should have happened?** Ask questions and listen carefully. Was perception a problem? What were they expecting?

**What went wrong?** This is where you start partnering with the client.

Keep in mind the true cost of an unhappy client. What future (life-time value) purchases could you expect from this client?

What future business could this client influence? What does the problem at hand cost to rectify? *Hint: average cost is 8-16 customers lost for each un-satisfied customer.* This can be expensive.

From experience, 'problems' generally often fall into 4 major areas:

**Mechanics or Function** - product or service failed to work as expected.

**Assembly or use** - someone didn't use it correctly or put it together incorrectly. ☺

**The People Factor** - we make mistakes in how we do something or how we deal with a client.

**Client EGO** - how this PROBLEM makes them look or feel (good or bad) in their eyes and the eyes of their friends and families.

**Stage Three: Explore and DISCUSS possible solutions.** This is possibly the most critical part in the client satisfaction/problem solving process.

Here is where we need to fully focus and *objectively* look at the challenge, we've partnered with the client to solve. Again, a few action steps. As a leader or coach, you can creatively follow this path with your team as well.

**Suggest options**. Take time to explore ALL the options that might effectively help solve this problem or at least minimize the impact.

**Ask your customer for their ideas and input**. Very often, they have a solution in mind, or have some good input that will help you mutually resolve it to their satisfaction. If they are a partner in the decision, they will help make it work and will be more inclined to be happier with the results. **Their satisfaction will result in ongoing referrals for you!**

**Agree on the best solution or course of action**. After you've fully explored the options, make sure you both agree on what and when you will do to resolve it. **THEN 'JUST' DO IT!**

**Stage Four: Act to resolve the problem.** This is the completion stage that builds a foundation for a potential long-term relationship with your formerly dissatisfied client. Make this a priority focus for your firm. Once you've agreed on what needs to be done, move heaven and earth to do it, and do it better and quicker than you've promised. Remember, they are watching to make sure you were *serious* about making them happy. This is your chance to prove your commitment. Learn to do it with a genuine response.

**Again, three action steps:**

**Physically remove the cause of the problem** or take steps to retrain if personnel.

**Take corrective action** to substitute, replace, or repair the product or service.

**Ask the client if they are satisfied** with the changes and action you've taken.

**Going the extra mile!** This is where you cement the relationship by doing something extra, something totally unexpected by the client. Show them you care and are concerned about the inconvenience they've experienced. **Apply your creativity to cementing the relationship!**

**Use your complaints as a creative source of product or service development.** Each one is an opportunity for you to learn how to better serve your clients, refine your service, or improve your product in the market place. This is also an opportunity to expand your business or service by using these creative solutions as stepping-stones or business building blocks.

**Yesterday's problems are today's new and improved products or services.** Want to be a creativity leader? YES! Then learn from each lesson your clients give you. This is an opportunity for you to build a strong foundation for success well into the next millennium. **Don't miss the lesson. It might be a "v-e-r-y" valuable one!**

**PRO-TIP:** Customers want to know how you can serve them, not how much trouble you are going to on their behalf. (By the way, in case you had forgotten, that's your mandate – serving the customer.) Making your customer feel valuable, not like a mere dollar sign, should be a no-brainer.

Through your own life experience, you know what you want as a customer/client. How can you translate that into what you provide as a business? To start with, here are a few simple practices:
• Listen to your customers/clients.
• Be helpful rather than obstructive.
• Go the extra mile to ensure your customers are satisfied.
© *Faith Wood*, *CSP* www.imind.ca

**PRO-TIP:** What if … people found ways to stay curious and open to new possibilities, to be as engaged as possible for as long as possible? This is entirely possible, if we become skilled at rekindling our sparks in the face of malaise. In the words of George Eliot, "It's never too late to be what you might have been."
© *Patricia Katz*, *CSP, HoF* www.patkatz.com

# Creative Freedom

Question everything? Does what you're doing...

+ Provide enhanced 'value' to the product or customer?
+ Improve 'quality'?
+ Improve 'productivity' or directly reduce costs?
+ Improve 'two-way communication'?
+ Improve 'service'
+ Add to employee satisfaction, 'motivation' or morale?
+ 'Empower' your employees to act?
+ Encourage 'innovation'?
+ Speed up the 'decision-making' process?
+ Give customers more 'reasons' to deal with you?
+ 'Free up time' to more productively sell or service?

What if it didn't exist?

Is it already being done by someone else?

Is it a 'valid' tradition? Why?

Can another person, department, or company do it better, faster, less expensively, or more
easily?

*Principles made personal yield powerful results - Ideas At Work!*

Creating the freedom, you seek will challenge you to look at where and what you are currently doing. These questions apply primarily to your career or business role, but many of them can be applied to your life. Answer wisely!

# Leadership skills (personal and positional)

## Leadership skills are changing; are yours?

**Leadership** *and working with teams can be fun. It can also be an exercise in futility and frustration, if done ineffectively.*

**Leading** *is an acquired skill in the art of working with people, helping them focus their efforts on a common goal or team objective.*

If you seek to be an **effective 21st century leader**, a reflective look at this list of leadership styles, activities, or attributes might be in order. Ask yourself how many of these you exhibit as you seek to lead those men and women who have entrusted you with their concerns and trust.

**What needs to change for you to become more effective in your leadership? Perhaps being more...**

## Responsible

Do you take full responsibility for your actions and decisions? Do you also take responsibility for their end results? Are you responsible, accountable, and available when decisions are made and needed steps taken by your team? True leaders take 100% responsibility for their lives and well-being on the job.

## Growth focused

Are you an *on-the-grow* leader, who is committed to seeking out new ideas, new methods, and new alliances to help serve those you lead? Are you a leader who is also a reader, actively seeking knowledge to help you lead?

## Exemplary

Do you walk your talk? Do your motives, actions, and attitudes reflect the person, the leader you would honestly like to become?

## Inspiring

Do you inspire confidence and trust in those who follow you? Can you call them to action in solving your mutual challenges?

## Efficient

Do you leverage your time as well as the time of those you serve wisely? Do they see you using your time in productive activities on their behalf? Do you have time to fully do your job? Do you make time to LEAD?

## Caring

Do your people know from *first-hand* experience that you care about them? Do you model it as you move through your day?

## Communicating

How are you at sharing your ideas, listening to the needs and concerns of your people, and making sure that you fully understand them? Do you make sure they are well informed about what the challenges and your proposed solutions to those changes entail?

## Competent

This strikes at the heart of your ability to deliver the goods for your people. Are you competent to do the job and do it well? What do you need to learn?

## Goal oriented

Are you a leader who is effective in setting realistic goals, communicating those goals, and gathering people to support the attainment of those common goals? A leader who achieves the worthwhile goals set for the common good.

## Decisive

Can you make an *informed* decision and *act* on that decision quickly? Or, do you study a challenge to death and continually put off deciding while waiting for more information?

## Unifying

Are you a leader who seeks to *include* everyone involved and works hard to make sure no one is excluded? Are you a leader who builds bonds between diverse groups with conflicting agendas and viewpoints? Are you a leader who can earn their trust and allow them to get past their divisiveness to get behind you in accomplishing something in everyone's best interest? Are you a creative catalyst for commitment and concrete action?

## Working

Are you a leader who is committed to working on behalf of those who trust you? A leader who is not afraid to get their hands dirty, dig in, and lead by example; to do what is needed to get the job done successfully? Are you a leader who sets an *energetic pace* and is fully engaged working out the solutions and to engaging people in the partnership of performance in achieving common goals?

**Challenging list, isn't it?** Yes, it is! But if you would truly seek to be a 21st century leader these are the skills that will assist you in successfully serving and leading your people.

## Are you willing to lead change?

# A question of leadership?

Leadership is an important skill for anyone wanting to create or enhance a successful career. Leadership can lead to recognition and open doors to your success working for yourself or someone else.

## Think about the following list of names.

| Meg Whitman | Jack Welsh | Walt Disney |
|---|---|---|
| Mary Kay Ash | W. Clement Stone | Warren Buffet |
| Eiji Toyoda | **YOU?** | Sam Walton |
| Fred Smith | Lee Iacocca | Bill Gates |
| Michael Dell | Clive Beddoe | Steve Jobs |

## Ask yourself:

- What do they have in common?
- What do you know about them and/or their companies?
- What connections or commonalities do they share?

## Now you might be thinking:

- Each of them started, built, or led a billion-dollar company employing thousands.
- Many started with very little capital, overcame struggles, and/or took on struggling organizations to re-create them and lead them to success.
- Each has gained national or international exposure and recognition for their leadership, success, and achievements.
- Each of them has become or was wealthy.
- Some have retired well or passed away.
- Most of them are male; only two are women.

**You would be correct.** However, the connections I've drawn are slightly different. Let's take a minute to remind you of the organizations each of these leaders created or led to greater success.

- Meg Whitman started an on-line company called **eBay.**
- **Mary Kay** Ash created the company that still bears her name
- Eiji Toyoda was part of the family who created **Toyota**
- Fred Smith launched **FedEx** which continues to deliver value

- Michael Dell started **Dell Computers** while still in college
- Jack Welsh was a legendary **GE** leader who created leaders and a very profitable, well-run company
- W. Clement Stone made his initial fortune in the insurance industry, but is best known for starting **Success Magazine** with Napoleon Hill; and hiring and mentoring motivational author **Og Mandino**
- Lee Iacocca took on the challenge of rebuilding **Chrysler** and saved them from bankruptcy
- Clive Beddoe was one of 4 founding partners with successful Calgary, AB based **WestJet**
- **Walt Disney** needs no introduction for his creative leadership
- **Warren Buffet** is still one of North America's savviest investors
- Sam Walton started a small store called **Wal-Mart** which grew to be the world's largest company
- Bill Gates created **Microsoft** and gave **Apple's** Steve Jobs someone to compete with ☺

*Bob speaking to 3200 grades 3-7 students at an anti-bullying rally*

Let me ask you two personal questions:

- Can you see *your* name included in the 'center' square at some time in your future? Yes? No? Why not?
- Do you see the *less obvious* connections?

Now you might be saying, "NO" to these questions. Some of you would say, ***"No way, Bob! I can't see 'MY' name included in this list of famous, influential, successful, and wealthy people."***

**Why not?** What is stopping you from being included at some time in your future?

- Each of these took **_personal leadership_** over their life and business careers.
- Each created something of **_definite value_** for those who joined them in their quest.
- Each exhibited definite attribute of **_true_** leadership and effective management, which propelled them to succeed in their respective ventures.
- **Each spelled their _leadership_ with multiple _P's_.** Their success and track record reinforce that observation. Each of them exhibited _all or most_ of the following traits (P's) in various degrees of intensity in their life and their leadership. None of them started out rich or famous.

Each of us can learn from their example, build on their expertise, and expand our personal leadership success. Can you begin to see a glimpse of yourself? Look at the characteristics (below) observed in their successful leadership. Let me ask you again. **_"Can you see yourself included?"_** Perhaps you are now saying, **_"Yes!"_** That is great!

Each of you has the capacity/potential to take personal leadership over your area and expand your leadership role. There is **not** one person reading this who has not exhibited some or these traits in various degrees or in specific situations. Wouldn't you agree? Ask your team?

**Leaderships' multiple Ps:**

- **Passion**
- **Purpose**
- **Principled**
- **Persistence**
- **Performance oriented**
- **Positive**
- **Perspective**
- **Persuasive**
- **People builders**
- **Pride of ownership**

Each of these traits can be honed and enhanced. Each of them is a learned and applied leadership success skill.

- What stops you from studying and working to enhance and expand your perspective and performance as a leader where you serve?
- What stops you from taking personal responsibility for your growth, involvement, and career success?
- What stops you from taking personal responsibility for your career and area of responsibility?

**Only you!**

So why not go for it?
Why not become that innovative leader?
Are you willing to step up and take on that leadership role?
Are you willing to be included in the list of people who continue to spell leadership with multiple P's?

**It's really a question of leadership.**

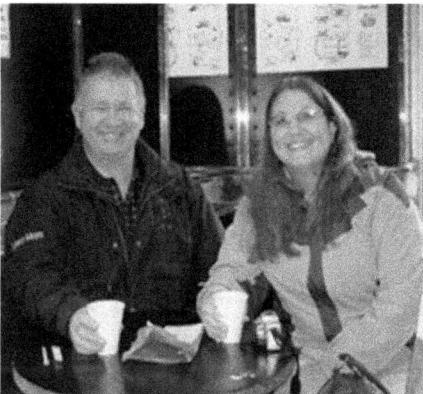

*My wife, Irene and I enjoying a coffee and croissants on the Eiffel tower. She met me in Paris on my way home from accepting an* **'Excellence in Innovation Award'** *and speaking in Mumbai, India. I'd suggested she meet me on my way home and celebrate her birthday week. She picked Paris and I got to visit this city that I learned to love for the first of several visits.*

*She is my partner on my leadership journey. Thanks Irene.*

**PRO-TIP:** Some of us have grown up believing that as a leader, not knowing the answer, making mistakes or asking for help is a sign of weakness. In fact, it's the contrary. **It takes a true leader to ask for help.** Doing this not only shows your humanity, it also gives those you lead an opportunity to shine and demonstrate their leadership themselves and to show that they too can have valuable input make a difference. Equally important, it also sends out the message that it's ok to ask for help. As 17th Century English author John Donne once said, "No man is an island."

© *Greg Gazin* www.gadgetguy.ca

33

# 12 key strategies for 'Bringing out the BEST in people'

*"Never, never, never, never, never give up!"* was the sage advice of **Sir Winston Churchill** in answer to how he successfully led the British people to withstand the might of the Nazi war machine. When faced with a leadership challenge, remember his words and dig in… amazingly enough when you do, so will your team!

**Alan Loy McGinnis** wrote **'The Time Trap'** in the last century about bringing out the best in people. It was well-received and gained exposure and acceptance among *progressive* leaders at that time. I've reflected on what he outlined and have his **'12 Rules'** sitting on the wall above my desk as this chapter was written. They serve as a *visual guide* and reminder of their importance in leading and coaching the people, *like yourself*, with whom I have the privilege of working with across North America and, more recently, around the globe.

If you are **committed** to be an effective leader, perhaps they should be sitting somewhere close, so they are not far from your mind's eye. They are included, along with my own reflective thoughts, for your **inspiration, information, and illumination.**

## Expect the best from the people you lead

See them performing at their best, even when they are struggling. People will often rise or fall to the level of our expectations and our coaching. See them as they could be, not as they are, at present!

**Don't limit them** by expecting or accepting less than their best. You owe it to them to set realistic, but challenging expectations. You can help them reach these as their coach, cheerleader, or champion. This can be a large challenge when you are a leader faced at working with what seems to be a dysfunctional or fractious team. Your saving grace can be keeping your eye and those you lead on the ultimate or shared goal.

*For example,* **General Eisenhower** *had the challenging role of being the supreme commander in the liberation of Europe during the Second World War. He faced an enemy who was well equipped and motivated to win. He also faced the challenge of working with warring factions within the Allied ranks. He persevered and went on to help us win.*

34

## Make a thorough study of the other person's needs

Each person on your team is an individual with specific skills, talents, strengths, weaknesses, needs, and dreams. Investing the time to get to know them makes it easier to lead and direct them for mutual success. Investing time in understanding and getting to know them also builds strategic bonds which can build bridges to the success and positive performance of them and your team.

**Weak leaders lead from the surface! Strong leaders dig deep** to learn what best motivates those they lead. They know where to best challenge and direct their skills for success. This allows them to best direct and use the talents and skills of their entire team.

## Establish high standards for excellence

Leaders *ultimately* fail when they accept mediocre results or neglect to set challenging standards. As mentioned previously, don't fail your team by allowing them to be *just* ok in their roles.

People will amaze you when you set the bar higher and lead by example. There are valid examples where good enough was appropriate. However, we settle for *seconds* (left-overs) when we could have reached higher, dug deeper, and been more successful. Be realistic but be ready to push past the comfort zone into the winner's zone. The example and standards you set and accept as a leader will determine the growth and success of your team.

## Create an environment where failure is not fatal

*Bob signing books & speaking in Kish, Iran*

Mistakes are a *natural part of life* and taking risks means occasionally you fail. If your team feels supported and encouraged, they will begin to take risks and move past their **comfort zone into the winners' zone**. Help them learn from the lessons of any mistakes and move ahead with energy to face the next challenge. Help them stretch and grow, knowing that they will make mistakes and grow in their journey, as you did!

35

*I remember having one of the clerics in my Tehran, Iran audience take me aside (firmly holding my arm) to talk about this. He talked about failure and being a martyr for God. I got more concerned as we talked. It was a tad nerve wracking time, for sure.*

*Eventually I said,* **"Seems like we are both saying we want our people to take risks."** *He nodded, and I quickly said goodbye and quickly walked away. Whew!*

## If they are going anywhere near where you want to go, climb on other people's bandwagons.

A *wise* leader is open to letting his team set the pace and direction, provided it takes them along the path towards the eventual goal set by the leader. In this case, you as the leader can become their cheerleader and coach, helping them move along more successfully. *I have frequently found team members had great ideas and their creative input moved us successfully forward.*

Sometimes, you need to be honest and realize that people are not going the same direction or share the same values as you. In that case, redirect them or let them go and stay your own course. Be courageous enough to realize that you can follow your own path. Others who share your values will follow.

### Employ strategic models to encourage success

This goes to the *heart* of leadership by example. Make sure this is modeled in your own life and in the lives of those you promote and delegate to succeed. When your team sees it working in your life and actions, they will be more open to allowing change in their own lives and performance.

### Recognize and applaud achievement

People do not work **simply** for money. In fact, most of the lists compiled show money much lower on the chart of motivators. Each employee or team member has his or her own needs, desires, and drives. Know them so you can strategically employ them and help them grow and succeed.

**Two of those needs, deep inside each of us are:**

1) The need to feel **appreciated** and important.
2) The need to feel **included** in the process.

As a leader, the most effective thing we can do is to recognize achievement and effort from those we lead and to share and applaud their achievements.

Often **small, genuine recognition activities will be more effective** than fancy reward programs. The point is to make sure you see what they are doing and let them know you appreciate it. **Hint:** Make sure any recognition is personal, timely, and relevant to their needs and desires.

## Employ a mixture of positive and negative reinforcement

We understand it is a good thing to provide praise and positive reinforcement in our team members' efforts. This affirms their actions and encourages them to move ahead. **Praise in public, correct in private!**

It is also necessary, at times, to apply the opposite tactic when one of them is doing something detrimental or self-defeating in the fulfillment or follow-through of their role. Letting them know what is **NOT** acceptable is part of a leader's role. We can do it nicely but do it we must; if they are to grow and maximize their potential. Correct in private as your goal here is to help them, not embarrass them.

## Appeal *sparingly* to the competitive urge

Each of us has a natural competitive edge. If used wisely, competition for personal growth and success can be a great tool to higher achievement. However, it has its *dark* side in allowing divisive actions and negative attitudes to creep into a team environment. Focus on the *team accomplishment* and mutual win. Encourage each team member to compete for higher standards and personal skill development.

## Place a premium on collaboration

This is where team 'works' and where effective leaders learn to pull people from diverse backgrounds, agendas, and experiences into an effective working unit.

Brainstorming is one way of effective collaboration and team building, allowing each team member to build and draw on the brainpower of another. What you are looking for is adding value vs. tearing down or unproductive criticism and negativity.

## Build into the group an allowance for storms

It is not always smooth sailing as a leader. Surprise, surprise! Storms, difficulties, challenges, detours, and disasters can strike when you least expect them.

*When we were sailing to Japan from Hawaii in September of 1988, we encountered what the Japanese later told us was a 'baby' typhoon. I'm sure glad it didn't reach puberty! ☺*

*Our captain was an experienced sailor and former US Coast Guard Captain. The other two crew members had deep water experience and had encountered similar storms (but not typhoons).*

*I had never experienced anything like this as most of my sailing was near coastal or island areas! I was more than a bit nervous, more so when we tipped the boat. ☺*

***Captain John's** commanding leadership, along with the hands-on experience of **Phil** and **Dave** helped us survive this life threatening super-natural phenomenon. After righting the boat, we fought the storm for over 13 hours before reaching safer sailing. We dealt with it as we needed to survive and to gain our port of Kobe, Japan.*

As a leader, you need to build in allowances for these *speed bumps, storms*, and *detours* in your team's progress and have plans in place to cover each potential challenge. Sometimes you need to step in and help them weather the storm.

## Take steps to keep your own motivation high

You are 'on' as a leader all the time. This means people will be looking at you and taking their cue from you. It also means you need to keep your personal motivation high and maintain a positive outward attitude (even when you don't feel it). This means you may need to find a trusted advisor or coach with whom you can discuss your challenges in private.

**Letting your negative feelings show can be devastating to your team.** They look to you as being confident, clear in focus, and consistent in action and follow through. Don't disappoint them! Understand and learn to apply these basic keys (rules) of the leadership road to smooth out your path and make it easier for those who follow you to successfully walk in your footsteps.

38

# Creating TIME for effective training

Investing in continual training and professional development allows your team the opportunity to fully realize their potential. It pays big dividends with better-equipped, energized team players on the job. As a top-level leader and team coach this can be your biggest time challenge as well as opportunity for success.

**Finding 'time' for your team members to attend training can be a challenge for most organizations.** Applying creativity to your training program can yield powerful results in their sales and customer recruitment and retention.

**These ideas will reduce excessive classroom instruction time**, without jeopardizing the process of quality face-to-face, interactive training:

- Schedule team members to attend training between 10AM and 3PM, instead of a full day. In this case, they can still attend to urgent business and client follow up. This works well for on-site training or training held very close to your operation.
- Weekend seminars and retreats are increasing in popularity. However, if you ask your team to sacrifice their private time, be sure to include some group outing or banquet to show your appreciation. Trade off time during the week would be nice too!
- Suggest your team study or read up on the course material in advance so they can hit the seminar running. Professional trainers can provide advance materials to facilitate this process.
- How about scheduling a 'lunch and learn' or 'breakfast briefing with Bob' by inviting in a local expert when your team needs information on a simple topic. Or combine a 'breakfast briefing' for management or specific team members in addition to half day or full day training.
- Visit: **www.ideaman.net** or **www.BobHooey.training** for more information on our programs and materials to assist you in enhancing your career or leading your team.

# How to avoid 'expensive' training mistakes

As a *leading-edge* owner, executive, manager, or team leader you may be asked to make decisions to engage or contract on programs and policies that will either help or hinder your team in reaching their goals.

You can avoid making *'major-career limiting-expensive'* training mistakes by considering a few ideas and side-stepping some of these mistakes that have minimized returns on training dollars. Unfortunately training dollars are ultimately wasted when leaders make some or all the following mistakes. You can easily avoid them!

## Failing to fully assess team needs

Perhaps you are teaching your team skills they already have? Team members don't need training 'just for the sake of training'. I've heard managers say, *"Even if they know this stuff – a refresher won't hurt them!"*

Sometimes that is true. I have been asked back to reinforce a program or to provide add-on sessions or coaching. *For example, a large construction firm just had me back to do the same session seven years later.* However, if not handled correctly, it can be counter-productive to your end goals or even de-motivating to your team.

### Here's a suggestion

Before you contract or launch any training program, conduct a needs assessment with your team. Work to establish a 'comprehensive list of skills' of current team members. This way you may discover what they already know and what they need (and hopefully want) to learn. Then, as you provide training, it will send a 'positive' message that reinforces the idea that you value their contributions and are dedicated to helping them increase and hone their skills. Training can be perceived as a 'punishment or a perk' depending on how you position or frame it. Make it a perk!

Strategically design your training programs to incorporate follow up reinforcement to enhance their effectiveness. Make that a vital part of your program and design it to ensure it is productive reinforcement not a perceived punishment. *I do this for my clients to help reinforce their investment.* Let them know you are committed to their growth and success in their roles.

## Thinking (wishfully) that training sessions will eliminate conflict

Leaders and managers sometimes think that training, especially training that focuses on team or relationship building, will eliminate conflict on the job. Some programs over emphasize teamwork at the expense of **'team-effectiveness'**. All team efforts need to be focused; task and relationship oriented. When sessions focus 'too much' on relationship building vs. team-effectiveness they lose impact and may become counter-productive.

Team building is a very important aspect of any successful business or organization. Make sure it is not 'sacrificed' in replacement for 'team-effectiveness'. Professional leadership is being able to work with people who may 'bug you' and being able to direct their efforts to help the team succeed.

### Here's a suggestion

Work diligently to ensure everyone on your team understands that *constructive* conflict is an important part of the team process. Without some creative conflict and honest difference of opinion, you get mediocrity. As someone once told me, *"The opposite of conflict is apathy, not peace and harmony."*

The secret is in not taking conflict as a 'personal issue' or a negative result in the process. Creative, constructive conflict can be a 'strategic' part of a positive process in making sure your team makes the right choice and (time permitting) fully explores 'all' the options and potential pitfalls.

**Visit: www.legacyofleadership.ca/bonus.htm** for a special gift to help you in your leadership journey.

## Thinking of training as a program vs. an on-going process

One of the challenges in training is the expectation that a half-day, full day or even a few days of training can change years of embedded habit. Research shows that shorter sessions, with reinforced follow-up, spread over a longer time result in better retention and long-range effectiveness. 'Short and often' rather than a one-time massive attack seems to work better.

This is one of the reasons behind the success of our spaced online video coaching and training programs like *Secret Leadership Tips* or our *Speaking for Success* on-line coaching series.

### Here's a suggestion

For your training to be effective, insights and ideas gained during programs must be quickly translated into action (**Ideas at Work!**) – actions that are reinforced by the leaders on your team.

Real development is never completed, as is the true essence of education. In our live interactive sessions, audience members are challenged to make a specific commitment to act on what they learn and to schedule those actions.

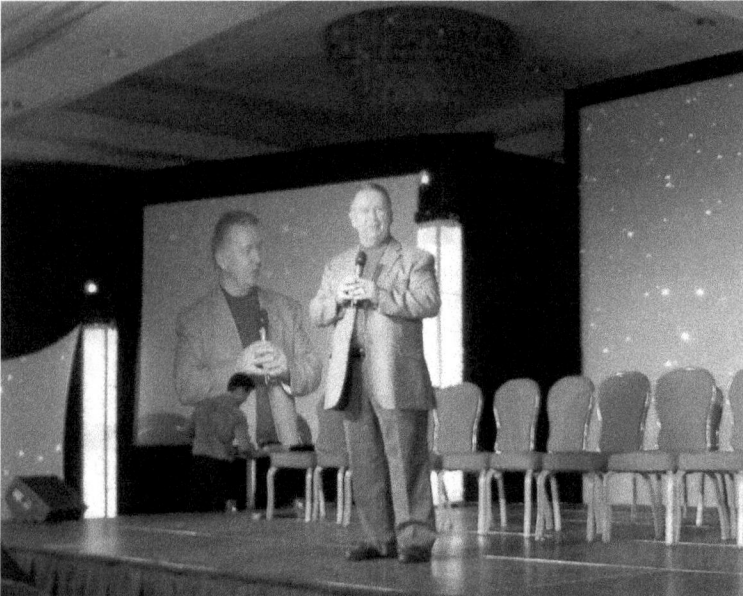

*Bob presenting at a CAPS annual convention a few years back*

**Visit: www.ideaman.net or www.BobHooey.training for more information on our innovative and pro-active training programs**

We trust these suggestions will help you as you search out the most effective training programs for your team. We'd be happy to share some other thoughts with you if you have any other questions or queries. Of course, we'd be happy to explore how 'we' might be of service in on-site training for you and your team.

*"My continued leadership growth and sharing of my leadership lessons are my gift back to them for the faith they showed in my life. Leadership is a 'giving back' lifestyle of choice and commitment."*
**Bob 'Idea Man' Hooey**

# Leadership observations

*"Learning is the essential fuel for leaders, the source of high octane energy that keeps up the momentum by continually sparking new understanding, new ideas, and new challenges. It is indispensable under today's conditions of rapid change and complexity. Very simply, those who do not learn do not long survive as leaders."*
**Warren Bevis & Burt Nanus**

These leadership ideas are drawn from observations and lessons learned first-hand from a wide range of leaders. I have been blessed with some great role models – leaders in business, industry, association management, community service, and Toastmasters; my NSA, GSF, and CAPS colleagues; and from my parents, my wife, and my friends. Here are some **shared characteristics** observed from the leaders in my life and experience.

## Leaders are not born

Leaders emerge and need to be nurtured by other leaders who see their potential. Leadership is a learned skill, honed by experience and by finding the inner motivational points that inspire people to assume leadership in various aspects of their lives. Leaders are *revealed* when people see value and follow their direction.

*I often saw this first-hand in my Toastmasters, NSA, and CAPS leadership roles. When I approached people, and asked them to tackle a challenge, they often took personal leadership and championed its eventual success.*

## Leaders are open to change

Leaders have the courage to lead change and to deal with change. Positive change often happens when someone takes personal leadership and responsibility in a situation and is open to grow.

Leaders develop a sense of adventure and a realization that change is not always a *negative* event. Leaders see themselves as catalysts for innovative and strategic change. A true leader will see the plateau or status quo as an opportunity or foundation to move ahead and make positive changes.

## Leaders are creative

Leaders are flexible to find solutions to common challenges. Often it is the creative approach that shows the way out of the problem or mess at hand.

This creative outlook may even create new products or entire industries. The leader looks for that creative or innovative *twist* which will unlock the secret to solving the challenge. They are persistent in looking for innovative ways to solve problems and will inspire others to do the same.

## Leaders make mistakes and build on lessons learned

Life is about learning and leadership even more so. Leaders take *calculated* risks and sometimes they make mistakes or fail. The difference being *true* leaders understand this and learn from the experience. This is a great part of the leadership process! Failure fuels their renewed determination to succeed. They will move ahead, better informed, striving for the next opportunity to 'lead and learn'.

## Leaders are forged in the heat of reality, moulded on the anvil of adversity, and formed by the hammers of life.

Personal leadership emerges in the heat of the worst challenges and conditions in your life. You can choose to take personal responsibility for your leadership role and abilities to act. I have seen the most unlikely men and women take this leadership role when the going was tough or the odds overwhelming – and succeed where others simply complained or quit trying. *President Lincoln's role was an example of this type of leadership challenge.*

## Leaders don't quit; they quietly find the strength and keep going.

## Leaders are more often avid readers

**This may not hold true of every leader.** However, many of those men and women I have grown to respect make *selective* reading a definite part of their leadership growth path.

They read outside their own areas of knowledge, experience, and industry. They are open to learn from a myriad of sources. They have found that in a multitude of counsel there is wisdom. *Fortunately for me, they are open to share it.*

Reading allows you to access the wisdom of the ages from leaders long gone as well as from current and emerging thought leaders. Selective, strategic reading and study provides value-added information that allows you to explore new ideas, new methods, and new ways of thinking. It gives you the leadership and career development ammunition you need to set, stretch, and successfully reach your goals.

Visit: **www.SuccessPublications.ca** for information on Bob's leadership, career, and business success publications.

## Leaders are the foundation upon which our success is given substance

*In my life, this is certainly true! I can look back to the pivotal points in my life and often there was the guiding hand of a leader who invested in my life, growth, and well-being.*

You might see parallels in your own life and career. So many men and women and organizations have played a role in helping me hone my talents and enhance my skills which allowed me to discover that I had hidden, un-tapped leadership strengths and skills.

I have been humbled by their investment, encouragement, and the recognition I have garnered along the way.

**PRO-TIP:** Lead from your heart, treat others with the same respect and compassion, patience and tolerance, kindness and optimism, as YOU would want to be treated. Start with 'relationship' then move to the 'tasks' at hand. 'Authenticity' is key. Connect heart-to-heart, side-by-side, even when you hold a higher position or status, remembering you're both 'fellow human beings' first.

© **Sheryl Roush**, *Accredited Speaker* www.SherylRoush.com

# Where are you going?

*"Only a clear definition of the mission and purpose of the business makes possible clear and realistic objectives. It is the foundation for priorities, strategies, plans, and work assignments. It is the starting point for the design of managerial jobs and, above all, for the design of managerial structures."* **Peter Drucker**

- What is driving you and your team?
- What is your defined purpose and strategic mission as an organization?
- What are you doing to engage and motivate your team to win?
- What are you doing to equip yourself and your team to win?

Funny how some non-structured time in the sun with a good book allows your mind to wander and wonder. Amazing how the warmth and sea air can stimulate your imagination and your ability to dream. The end of your next quarter is a good time to pause and reflect on how you and/or your team are doing. Remember those goals you set late last year or early this year?

*I found myself rethinking 'what I do' and 'why I do it' on a trip to Cancun. I had a wonderful time addressing the dealer/owners of a Canadian national tire chain. They were very receptive and open to challenge their own experiences and to revisit 'why' and 'what' they were doing. This, I believe, is the beginning of building strong, long-term foundations for profitable success under any organization. I hope my time with them will lead to additional opportunities to serve them and work with their organization. They are a great team of people!*

From personal experience, having a *"strongly defined"* visual image of your purpose and a strategic mission of what you do will keep you focused. It will keep you fired up and excited about your business and career. It will help you ride the tough times and challenges that come with everyday life and modern-day business.

**My challenge for you** is to take a minute... ok, 15 minutes, and take a serious look at what you are doing.

**Ask yourself:**

- Why are you doing it?
- What real value do you bring to your industry, market, and clients?
- What are you willing to change to make it better, more attractive, and value-added to your team and your customers?

PS: My personal (*separate from my professional one*) mission statement includes scheduling some winter 'Sun Time' to recharge my batteries, have fun, and relax on occasion. Even nicer when I can combine it with the work that I love. (*Just came in from ploughing about 2 feet of snow off my driveway. Gee, what a difference a week makes.*)

---

## Why should you have a mission statement?

Effective mission statements are not so much written on a piece of paper or on a poster but written in the minds and exhibited in the actions of you and your staff. **Ask yourself:**

- Is it something that all your team/staff had input in developing and agree with its aims?
- Is it clear and concise to make it easy to remember?
- Is it visible for customers and staff alike to see while in the work environment? If not, WHY NOT!

**"Our mission at Ideas At Work is to profitably provide our clients with life-proven, idea-rich, practical programs in personal and professional effectiveness.** (Innovative, engaging programs and materials will enhance their quality of life and advance their careers and effectiveness in their personal, business, or community involvements.)" We'd love to help you and your teams!

---

**PRO-TIP:** Our goals only really come alive and dance in our hearts and minds when we share them with others. We all need cheerleaders, those who lovingly applaud our success and challenge us when we lose sight of what matters most. Share your wildly important goals with those you trust, respect and love. Invite them to be an important catalyst for your success. Dream big, dream often, and let others experience that dream with you!
© *Linda Maul*, PCC linda@accountabilitybydesign.com

# Personal/professional productivity skills

## P*R*I*O*R*I*T*I*E*S

*"A hundred years from now it will not matter what size my bank account was, the sort of house I lived in, or the kind of car I drove... but the world may be different because I was important in the life of a child."* Anonymous

One helpful suggestion in your life and time management would be investing time to **ensure you are 'crystal clear' on your priorities** in life and business. Remaining focused on the priorities in your personal and family life makes it easier to balance and blend them with the demands of your business, community, and career priorities. Far too many of us have personally paid the price for being *unbalanced in our priorities* and have lost partners, careers, and families. These needless personal tragedies could have been avoided, if we'd only wisely invested the time!

*Someone challenged me, that to be truly effective in my life I should begin to* **'schedule my priorities instead of just prioritizing my schedule'.** *This subtle change in focus has made a major difference in its results and the accompanied lifestyle benefits.*

Knowing what your priorities are, and scheduling specific time each week to work on them brings freedom. **It helps you say 'NO!'** to demands that don't fall in line or would distract you from seeing your priorities fulfilled. You are better informed and able evaluate decisions, time investments, resource allotments, and specific goals. You can become more productive when you are working on the important projects in your career. You become more fulfilled when you spend time with the important people in your life.

Spending a few moments on a regular basis revisit and revise your priorities would be helpful!

## PLAN monthly, SCHEDULE weekly, and LIVE/LEAD daily!

Take a moment and make a note to yourself (yes, right here in YOUR book) about these various areas and your priorities. Spend time later to refine and focus your thoughts. Keep your written priorities clear, concise, and focused. Keep them visible as you go through your day.

The following five have helped me keep focused. Update them regularly. Ask yourself, **"What is the 'single' most important activity I can do this week or today to help me strategically reach my goals in 'this' area?"**

**FAMILY:**

**SELF-IMPROVEMENT:**

**CAREER:**

**COMMUNITY:**

**SPIRITUAL/SPORTS/HOBBIES:**

*I routinely schedule my 'focused five' activities. I take a careful look at my goals, intentions, and areas of concern and schedule the five most important activities first. Then I schedule the remainder of my activities. That way, I can make important activities my focus as I work through my week. This has made a tremendous difference in my leadership and overall productivity!*

**You might want to add a few more areas or redefine them to help make it more focused for you.**

**LEADERSHIP:** (specific to enhancing your skills and enhancing your productivity)

**WORK:** (separate from career)

**PERSONAL:** (separate from family and others)

If you've taken the time to fill out this section (and I trust you did) I'd like to commend you. Did you realize that you have now done what 95% of your fellow North Americans/global citizens never have? Most North Americans/global citizens have never taken even a few minutes to look at their lives and give some serious thought to their goals and values. Any wonder why their lives have been less than productive and fulfilling!

This time of *strategic* reflection and refocus can be a pivotal point in gaining effective control of your time and life. Please take the time to pause and ponder your priorities. It is worth it!

**PRO-TIP:** The biggest and most common mistake that I've seen speakers make is that they put most of their effort into selling their work. They believe that their primary job is to sell speeches. This strategy ignores the fundamental truth that it is the quality of our work that drives our success, and that if you want more work, you should focus on improving the speech. There isn't a business in the world that is more driven by customer word of mouth than the speaking business, and it is the quality of our work that determines whether that word of mouth is positive, neutral, or negative. If a speaker doesn't have enough work, the most dangerous and counter-productive thing he or she can think is, "It's not my speech. My speech is great. I just need someone to sell my speech." No.

If your speech was great, then word of mouth would drive business to you. Of course, we all need to market and sell to some extent, but the greatest sales booster is to constantly work on improving the quality of your work. Make the speech better. When it's good enough, the sales will come. Then you must always continue to make it better. Your success will be assured.
© *Joe Calloway*, CSP  www.JoeCalloway.com

# Time management needs to be an 'integral' part of your life

The tips and idea-rich techniques we discuss in *'Running TOO Fast'* or cover in more detail in our on-site interactive programs will be minimized without grafting a serious commitment and continuous action in time management into your life and work activities. They will work, but only if you apply them! We've excerpted a few tips for you.

**"If time and priority management is not an 'integral', daily part of what you '*are*' doing; all the technology/tools, as well as these idea-rich strategies and time management success systems will be wasted."**

Many of you are already 'jamming' too much into your hectic workweeks. The tendency for some of you will be to use these tools to crowd or load even more on your plate. This is counterproductive to the whole process. *As mentioned, too many people will seek to do just that. I did until I burned out. Then I started looking for ways to free up my time and leverage my abilities.*

The purpose here is to challenge you to decide what you 'value' and then create and schedule time for those activities and people you value. For some of you, this may be a welcome refresher and pat on the back for your efforts to bring your lives into balance and to make your career and business less of an intrusion.

For some, this may fly in the face of what you've been taught or even the expectations of the environment in which you find yourself currently engaged or employed.

Please trust me when I tell you, it is all about finding a sense of *'flexibility'*, balance, and purpose and then applying that to being more productive in your life. Your career is only a part (arguably, a larger time commitment) of who you are and what you will do with your life. Ensure that you factor in the important people in your life, as well as time to reflect and time to play and recharge your emotional and physical energies. Invest your time wisely, it is all you have.

Here are some **time-tested tips, techniques, and principles** to make effective time management a part of your life.

- Use a master task or **'big picture'** list. Update, review, replace, and amend as needed to keep this current.

Use this master list as a tool for your long-term planning efforts and to keep track of what you want to do, or promised to do. Then schedule accordingly to best use your time to fulfill your promises and to move your life and career ahead productively.

- Develop a '**STOP DOING List**' of items you are determined to eliminate in your life and work.
- Invest at least 5-10 minutes in pre-planning for each day. Refer to the big picture list and see where these items might fit in your daily schedule.
- Carry over 'essential' items from your previous day's list; but remember, schedule wisely to avoid overbooking, or overload.
- Design a **'Someday list'** as a place to park activities you can use as productive fillers while waiting.
- Design in **flexitime** for life's little surprises. You know - the things that get in the way of your plans. I've learned to never schedule more than 50% of any day which leaves flexible time for fill-ins.
- Use the method Andrew Carnegie paid a consultant $25,000 to learn. Rank tasks as A, B, or C's. A's to be done today, B's will soon move into the A category, and Cs are 'done' only when you have extra time. Often, the C's can be deleted or delegated without any loss or even being noticed. This works to help you set priorities and then schedule them accordingly.
- **Break larger projects into smaller ones** and do a line chart with real deadlines for accomplishments. Put those deadlines and checklists in your day timer or on your electronic calendar so they remain visible. Focus your efforts and work towards specific manageable tasks. Can you delegate some of them? As a leader, you simply cannot do everything. Think strategically and delegate effectively where applicable!
- Handle each piece of paper, phone call, or email only once, if possible. Apply the 3 Ds of time management: deal with it, delegate it, or dump it!
- **Apply the 2-minute rule:** If it can be done in 2 minutes or less – do it now!
- Use on-the-spot notes and documentation to adjust your priorities as needed. **Do it NOW!**
- Understand and use your energy levels and schedule for maximum output. Understand your biorhythms for best results. Know when your best time of the day is for creative, or brain challenging work and schedule those activities accordingly.

# Would an extra 8 to 10 hours per week of recaptured or repurposed time:

- **Make a difference in your workday?**
- **Make a difference in your productivity?**
- **Allow time for more training and effective delegating?**
- **Help you with career advancement?**
- **Help you enrich your family time and relationships?**

*I frequently share these additional **'time nudges'** with our audiences and readers with encouragement to explore them to see if they fit in their situation. Each of them works to free up or create at least 10-30 minutes a day by better use and leverage of your time and/or by eliminating or minimizing time wasters. Some even more! Not all of them will fit your use, but you might still glean an idea or two from each one.*

**15 minutes a day works out to approximately 91 hours over a year.** 30 minutes a day is equivalent to 178 hours or 4.5 weeks. WOW! Perhaps, you can see where you might be able to better invest that recaptured time to grow yourself, your career, your team, or your business. Each can be explored and applied in less than 60 seconds. Good luck in your quest to regain control and leverage your time to be more productive. These small *'seemingly insignificant'* minutes, reclaimed and invested wisely over your life, could easily give you the equivalent of an 'advanced' education in a field of your choosing.

**Would this make a difference in your career path? I would say YES!**

- For example: if we read an average of twelve pages a day (about 15 minutes), we could easily read 17-18 business or leadership books per year. Considering the North American average is ONLY ONE NON-FICTION BOOK PER YEAR - you might begin to see the competitive advantages of investing 15 minutes a day in self-study.

- I've heard it said that, *"In one year, any one of us could become a local authority in our chosen field of study, in less than three years an expert, and potentially, in just under five years, an internationally acclaimed authority in that particular field of study."* Works for me!

- We enjoy a definite advantage or edge for success when we are well read. Reading BROADENS our experience, expertise, and expands our possibilities. Sadly, statistics show that approximately 40% of North American adults are not 'fully' capable of reading even their daily working material. Investing as little as 15 minutes a day could effectively teach them the fundamentals of reading and make a major impact in their lives and their employment prospects. We, as leaders, could make this happen!

- Alternatively, these same 'insignificant' minutes could help us get into and stay in shape while tuning up our heart. I'm told just 15 minutes of cardio-vascular (aerobic) activity - 3 times a week is all we really need to maintain a healthy body. Maybe take the stairs if it is less than two floors? INTERESTING! Only 15 minutes you say. Hmm, maybe tomorrow? ☺

- Perhaps these 'insignificant' minutes would well be spent or invested in personal meditation or spiritual contemplation, helping to bring your soul, mind, and spirit into balance.

- Maybe, these 'mini-moments' could be shared exclusively with your family or close friends engaging in real, quality communication to create and build healthy life-long relationships?

*"Don't waste time,"* writes Australian pioneer **Arthur Brisbane**. *"Don't waste it regretting the time already wasted... you have time enough left (for some accomplishment and recovery) if you will but use it... while life and time remain."*

**Your life and time management are 'truly' in your hands.** It is within your power to choose to invest it well for your benefit and the benefit of those you love and with those you lead. Or you can choose to let others rob you of your life's blood or squander it on useless pursuits. It is your choice - and it's about time!

**Potential savings from making effective Time Management a focus: 30-60 minutes per day**

**PRO-TIP:** For years I've told my audiences - and my children - about the two fundamental truths I've discovered which pave the way to success. First, intentionally and consistently seek out and *do the things* others could have done -- probably should have done - but consciously chose not to do. Second, pursue the hardest, most intimidating tasks first. Remember, the greater the sacrifice, the harder it is to give up - and the sweeter the ultimate reward!

© *Phillip Van Hooser,* MBA, CSP, CPAE  www.vanhooser.com

# A 60 second time nudge (productivity tips)

Here are some quick reminders of effective ways to be more productive and make better use of your time. If you are a busy leader or manager, these will help. Are you being serious about increasing your effectiveness personally or as a leader and/or your income through building your business and team and finding ways to profitably create repeat customers? They will provide solid guidance to increased effectiveness and productivity.

Consistent application in using your time wisely will allow you to free up time for face-to-face interaction with current and potential clients; as well as working with employees to allow more time for the leadership and management process. This 'liberated' time can be leveraged in investing in equipping and motivating your team to win. Lead by example and get your team to apply these reminders to help them be more effective.

## Strive for flexibility and balance

Above all in the process of learning to effectively leverage your time, strive to find and maintain a flexible balance between your personal and business time. This is crucial to your long-term success! This is the only way you will find a sensible path that allows you to be productive, make the necessary changes needed to regain control of your life, and not burn out yourself, your colleagues, or your family members.

*Potential savings from making Self/Time Management a focus: 30-60 mins per day*

## Strive for personal organization

Keep focused on what is an important 'priority' for you in each area of your life and career. **Create your personal 'Focused Five'** list (where you outline the 'single' most important decision/action that will move that area or priority productively ahead. (See page 49 for more information). Start each day with time focused on planning and scheduling what is truly-of-value for that day. Schedule your priorities!

**Remember** to schedule around your personal energies to ensure the most important and creative activities are scheduled for that time when you are at your best. Time management is really a personal leadership choice!

*Potential savings from better organization: 15-20 mins per day*

## Configure your office for maximum productivity

Your on-site productivity starts with making sure your working environment is ergonomically designed and organized. Reduce the chances of repetitive strain injury (RSI) or long-term loss of energy by ensuring things are within easy reach and located where they offer you the best efficiency. *Over the years, I have learned the value of a well-organized work place where I can easily access and find what I need without needless wasted time.* This one area alone can free up large blocks of time, a minute here and a minute there.

*Potential savings from better use of design: 10-30 mins per day*

## Learn and leverage using technology

With the advent of improved and cost-effective computers, printers, software, office networks, cell phones, etc. we finally have access to a group of tools we can use to free up and/or leverage time. If you are looking for a competitive edge, you will find it by exploring and expanding your use of technology to systemize your business and reduce the repetitive activities to a minimum.

This is an area where you can design systems or access apps and programs which will allow you to free up and leverage larger increments of time. Leveraging this area has allowed me to expand my ability to create programs and products to better serve my audiences and clients around the world.

*Potential savings from leveraging technology: 15-30 mins per day*

## Use your website wisely

The smarter business leaders are learning how to more fully unleash the power of the Internet and harness the power of their websites by turning them into virtual assistants. Use your website as a client service tool, an information and resource base for potential and current clients; one that can show your potential clients the depth and scope of your skills, services, and commitment to their success.

*Our **www.ideaman.net** website was revamped to do that, and it is paying for itself every year with client contact and contracts. We asked North America's top experts to share their thoughts in **'A Creative Collection of Wisdom and Writing'.***

*We expanded our meeting planner section to aid and offer free downloadable meeting and conference checklists, tips, and techniques from the experts. We've added resource articles to* **www.BobHooey.training, www.AlbertaSpeakers.com,** *sites as well. Invest a few minutes to review some of the articles we've included from experts around the globe.*

*Potential savings from web wisdom: 15-30 mins per day*

## Use your email effectively

Investigate ways of harnessing email to provide ease of access to clients, using autoresponders to answer common questions and develop more effective ways of maintaining and initiating a true *two-way communication* with your suppliers, colleagues, and clients.

Allocate specific times to access and respond to your email. Limit replies to one per minute. Use spam filters and create rules (which move regular emails from one source to a folder for later reading. Create contact groups for group emails. Create folders for newsletters and other regular emails. Read later!

*Potential saving from better use of email: 15-30 mins per day*

## Maximize leveraging time by collaboration

As you learn to leverage your time, do what other successful business leaders are doing in increasing numbers – find and engage outside help. Use the services of a virtual or real-time assistant. Look for ways to outsource repetitive and non-revenue generating and marketing activities. Perhaps you can work with a partner or colleague and share the load or engage a part timer who is tasked to free you up for those activities which potentially put you in front of those who can hire or buy from you.

*Potential savings from not doing it alone: 15-30 mins per day*

## Leverage your marketing/promotion with assistance from others

*Many years ago, I returned from our annual Canadian Association of Professional Speakers convention after investing a weekend with 340 fellow speakers, trainers, and facilitators. One of the speakers reminded us that we were first a marketer, secondly a businessperson, and thirdly a speaker. If you are not marketing, you are marking time; and if so, it is only a matter of time until you are marked for failure. Great advice for any industry!*

Focus on the most productive form of marketing and promotion – your sales and service efforts. Each client you sell and then successfully satisfy can become a marketer for you and your services. Each client who continues to visit or do business with you can become a fan and champion on your behalf. Ask for help in the other areas, such as networking, advertising, direct marketing, and public relations.

*Ten years ago, I created the first of a series of online joint venture promotional websites as a contribution to helping some of my colleagues work together to better reach our potential clients.*

**www.AlbertaSpeakers.com** has been very successful over the years, as have the other joint venture promotional websites

***Potential savings from better marketing efforts: 10-30 mins per day***

## Leverage your time by better use of outside services

When you are busy and productively investing your time in the service process, make sure you work to minimize other activities that would distract you or deplete your time and/or energy. This one might be a more personal tip to free you up for more productive investment of time in your career role or in a leadership role in equipping your team to productively grow.

Look for ways to offload personal activities using shopping services, personal assistants, cleaning services, etc. Harness the Internet to its full advantage for services and products you need for your business and personal life as well. Many office supply services will deliver to your desk if your order meets certain levels. Amazon does too. When you consider the time and expense of shopping personally, it just doesn't always add up.

***Potential savings using available services: 15-20 mins per day***

## Plan monthly (or quarterly), schedule weekly and LIVE daily!

*I have been preaching this focused formula around the world for the past 20 plus years. My experience and those of thousands of my readers and audience members has been to use this formula as a strategic freedom tool. (68 countries as of 2023)*

- When you know what is truly important to you and am clear and honest with your values, you can say **'NO'** to things that do not fit priorities and say **'YES'** to those who do.

- Take regular time either monthly or quarterly to think, reflect, dream, and then focus to gain freedom and to see your life become more productive, flexible, and balanced.

- Take the results of that process one step further and use that information to schedule specific time for strategic activities on a weekly basis to systematically achieve your goals.

- Personally, it frees me up to live and better enjoy my life *(on and off the job)* daily. I would hope it would serve that purpose for you.

## One more tip in using your time wisely: Manage the mornings!

My wise friend **Wayne Cotton** challenged me to 'manage my mornings'. If it is important and crucial to your success and long-term growth – schedule it and tackle it first thing in the morning. Then move on to whatever else needs to be done. That way, 'when' life happens, (and it does) you have already accomplished your most important activities and 'high value' priorities.

This list of reminders or **time 'nudges'** can help keep you on track as you seek to grow yourself and your team to the next level. Accomplishing this challenge will demand your continued diligence in getting the best results or 'payback' from your investment of time and resources.

Investing those resources and the 'liberated' time with your team will help you reach this success. More importantly, as you use these nudges to free up or recapture time (5 to 15 min blocks) make sure you know where you are going to reinvest this newly *found* time. As mentioned, deciding in advance where you will reinvest is a strategic success move and one that will enhance your abilities to grow and to leverage your time for increased success and profitability. It will also allow you to inject a bit more fun in your life too!

*SUMMARY: Total potential time savings*

What this means, conservatively, is we stand to gain at minimum 2 full hours per day by better planning, leveraging, and strategic use of our time applying some of these ideas.

**As leaders,** this is critical to your success and having the time for interaction, strategic training, and leading your teams. This could be the most 'value-added' activity you could do as a leader.

As a leader, would it be valuable to be able to invest the time in encouraging your star performers and coaching those who can be developed into stars? YES!

**As professionals**, these time savings, when re-invested in marketing efforts, will dramatically raise your profile, your profits, and the quality of your life style. Scheduling creative time to think, plan, and set new strategic initiatives into action is critical to your ongoing career growth and success.

*Flexibility is part of maintaining a sense of balance in life!*

**This 'recaptured' time**, when wisely re-invested, repurposed, and leveraged in the management process, gives a nice return on your efforts. Even if you were only able to average a better use of time resulting in two additional hours in only four of your five workdays, you would effectively free up eight hours. This would potentially double your time with clients, which could double your business as well as enhance your productivity. It would also open time to effectively engage your team members and help them grow to better success.

**Pause for a few minutes and reflect on your answers to the following questions in relation to 'your' recaptured time.**

• Would that 'recaptured' time make a difference in your take home pay this year? How much?

- Would that 'repurposed' time make a difference in your overall production and enhance your career or advancement potential?

- Would that 'refocused' time make a difference in your team's performance figures for the year? How much? Be specific!

- Would it make sense to continue systemizing processes or engaging the process of 're-designing' your work environment to free up this time?

- Are there areas where you can tighten up or re-design your schedule to free up time? Jot them down.

- Would some of these tips help members of your team to free up their own time for more productive use?

- Can you see the value this time leverage might have for you personally in your current leadership role?

- Would this allow you to spend more time training and delegating to free up even more tactical time for strategic use?

- Would this 'reclaimed' time allow you to invest quality time with your family and friends to build and enhance your relationships?

- Would this 'newly found' time allow you to inject more flexibility and fun into your life?

- What is stopping you from making these timely changes?

**PRO-TIP:** The next time someone challenges a core belief you hold, try being curious instead of furious.

*He says the sky is red. But I know it's really blue. They taught me that in the second grade. I can look out the window right now and see blue sky. So why does he believe the sky is red...?*

Curiosity comes from inquisitiveness, and being inquisitive is a foundation for creative thinking. By their very nature, brilliant entrepreneurs question everything. "Why is everyone doing it that way?" "Why can't it be done?" "I know it's impossible, but if it were possible, how could we do it?"
© ***Randy Gage*** www.randygage.com

# 4 P's of personal performance

I've had the privilege of traveling across North America and the globe, sharing my thoughts and seeing my **Ideas At Work** on how to regain control of your life, leadership, and time. I've been able to share with leaders, just like you, and heard their creative ideas and suggestions on how to effectively tackle the problems and time wasters we commonly face.

*"He who every morning plans the transactions of that day and follows that plan carries a thread that will guide him through the labyrinth of the busiest life. But where no plan is laid, where the disposal of time is surrendered merely by chance of incidence, chaos will soon reign."*
Victor Hugo

I hear leaders telling me, **"…life is good; but, out of control, over-committed, and with a blurring lack of focus on the important things and people in their lives."** Sound familiar?

**Is there really an answer?**

- Can we really take back control in this increasingly fast-paced world of Internet, cell phones, and other forms of **instant communication?**
- Can we balance our financial needs with our need for job, leadership, and family satisfaction?
- How do we balance our drive for personal and professional success with a need to **live our lives?**
- How do we create time to lead?

*"Success is not about money; it's about what you feel about yourself, your life, your friends, and your loved ones,"* shares former Success Magazine CEO **Peter Morris**. *"My friend, **happiness, success, and enjoyment come from a balanced life,** where material and spiritual values are viewed in perspective. The most profound success derives from the consistent application of your natural skills and energy in work that constantly challenges you to expand your horizons. **Get a life!"***

**The key here,** as Peter said, **is the word balance and a sense of flexibility.** All too often we find our lives in an unbalanced situation. This causes the negative stress on our lives, our families, and our career. **But how do we regain this balance?** The real secret is *simply* in how we portion out our time.

We've experimented with new ways of looking at and blocking out my time. The results of this research are what we call the **4 P's of Personal Performance**.

This planning process will, if applied wisely, help you re-focus your energies and resources in setting and achieving those worthwhile goals and the real desires of your heart. As a leader, please take heart, **you can gain freedom** by applying these techniques, along with the other ones we share in our programs and publications.

Our days can be more effectively used if we focus, plan, or block out our time, based on what we now call the **4 P's of Personal Performance**. In brief, **here they are.**

**PEOPLE/PAY DAYS:** Our success in life, leadership, and business is often directly related to our ability to relate and work effectively with other people. As leaders, our success is very dependent on maintaining good working relationships with our co-workers, employees, employers, suppliers, competition, and, most importantly, clients.

Simply put, **a people/pay day** is one where the *major* time focus is on finding, building, and maintaining the relationships that are important in your life, leadership, and business. Investing time nurturing and augmenting these relationships can work miracles in team building, client loyalty, and business longevity. **Hint:** For the serious, effective leader, at least a part of each day should be invested in this quest to better understand, support, and equip your team to win!

**POWER/PAPERWORK DAY:** There are days when the deadlines, the commitments, and the process of running our business and career just must be our *major* time focus. Rightly so! The work must be done, the business must be managed, and the invoices and orders must be processed.

**Power/Paperwork days**, are the days in which **we set aside blocks of uninterrupted time** to focus on specific projects or obligations and work through to make sure they are completed properly and on schedule.

**Days, when the work must be about the work – really do WORK! Hint:** As a leader, this is where more effective direction and delegation come into play, so you are freed up to accomplish your most important priorities and focus on your *vital* (only you can do) functions.

**PAUSE/PLAY DAY:** There are days when we need to regenerate, relax, take a break from our labours, enjoy our families, and sometimes daydream or even goof-off. Days in which we have fun, not focused on building a business, or in pursuit of training that will advance our leadership careers.

Maybe we take a **fun** course in something unrelated to what we do – just for the **joy of learning.** Maybe we take part of an afternoon off and sit quietly on a swing, or at the beach, watching the clouds as they slowly meander across the sky.

**Pause/Play days** allow us to reflect and refocus our energies, priorities, and resources; and help **make life worthwhile!** They are most effective in helping us regain control and in balancing our power and people days to maximize our effectiveness. **Hint:** Build this into your current leadership agenda. **Darren Hardy** recently told me, *"As leaders, we should get paid to rest, to pause. Our role is not defined by what we do, but often by what we don't do."* He suggested a process of **Sprint and Recover** where we work on one focused priority in 90-minute jam sessions and then allow ourselves to catch up or re-energize.

**PLANNING/PREP DAY:** These are day's allocated, monthly or quarterly, to work **ON** your business or leadership, not **IN** the business. Days when the *primary* time focus is on strategic planning, analysis, and other functions of a long-range perspective. **Hint:** This is crucial as you seek to *liberate* time to become a more effective leader and help guide your team to more productivity and success.

## Plan monthly, schedule weekly, focus, and lead daily!

That is not to say that you may have some weeks or days in which this isn't feasible, or you are working your way out of being over-committed. There are days when you will only be able to accomplish a part of your goal to schedule a people day, a pause day, or a power day.

*ReThink & ReTool Creativity*

It is important to have a guideline to assist in effectively laying out your life and commitments. Having a guideline also helps keep you focused and working toward your optimum effectiveness.

**Enjoy your life and choose to truly live, to effectively lead each day!**

## Reminders to help you regain your balance and enjoy life

- Just because you have the 'skill', **does not** mean you have the time! **Learn to say NO! In fact, this is one of your most important lessons if you are serious about creating time to lead.**

- Filtering your commitments through your life priorities can be a very effective tool against over commitment. **Ask yourself, "Is it 'really' important for 'ME' to do this?"** (Don't do – Delegate!)

- What activities can you eliminate, delegate, or ignore to free up time for the vital leadership activities and people you really value in life? **What's stopping you from being more effective?**

- 5 minutes spent each day on pre-planning can save you hours in leveraged productivity. **Plan and then do!**

- 15 minutes daily invested in self-study or reading in your field of expertise can give you a major, idea-rich, competitive edge in your career. **A major investment that pays off big time!**

- Use your day timer or electronic organizer as a strategic planning tool to *block out* time for leadership development, family, planning, fun, commitments and deadlines, creative time, and time for yourself. **Control is a process of strategic planning**. It is a **foundation for success in living** and in seeing our lives become fulfilled and productive.

I welcome your ideas on how we can make it work even better.

I've included these Leadership videos as a bonus for our readers. Simply follow the link to access them: **www.SuccessPublications.ca/Leaders-Tips.html**

**PRO-TIP: Dress for Success!** Your personal appearance and grooming have a profound effect on the visual delivery of your speech. Your audience will need to believe in you before they will consume your message. Therefore, present yourself appropriately for the culture of your audience. This will show you respect them, and it will build your credibility. They will now be able to hear what you have to say because your appearance is not a distraction to your message. Most countries now accept Western World business styles as appropriate.

© *Shirley Borrelli, B.Ed. Image Consultant* www.ShirleyBorrelli.com

# Identifying and eliminating your time wasters

Over the years, we've asked our audiences about their time challenges and been able to identify their **25 biggest time wasters.** Here they are!

1. Telephone interruptions
2. Failure to plan
3. Attempting TOO much
4. Drop-in Visitors
5. Socializing and daydreaming
6. Ineffective delegation
7. Travel (commuting)
8. Lack of self-discipline
9. Inability to say NO!
10. Procrastination - 'busy' work
11. Family concerns
12. Paperwork (where is the paperless office they promised me?)
13. Leaving tasks unfinished
14. Not enough staff or personnel
15. Meetings (unnecessary or unproductive)
16. Confused responsibility (I thought you were going to do _____?)
17. Poor verbal and written communication skills
18. Inadequate controls, feedback, or progress reports
19. Inaccurate or incomplete information
20. Personal and corporate disorganization
21. Email, texts, etc. (great if targeted and used appropriately)
22. Management by CRISIS!
23. Cell phones, i-pads, and tablets (they can be great if used properly)
24. Television
25. Surfing the Internet, Facebook, Twitter, etc. (Ok, I get caught up on it too!) www.ideaman.net

**You may have some of your own time wasters, not on this list. Time wasters take away from your high priority time as an innovative, effective leader.**

Take a moment to honestly appraise your life and leadership activities. Our audiences and leadership clients across North America have helped us come up with some novel approaches to help combat them.

**Go through the time wasters list.**

- Check off the time wasters you recognize (and remember the people who employ them against you) as draining your schedule and energy.

- Identify the major ones that are hurting your ability to successfully handle your leadership role!

- Decide to work on each one until you've eliminated or at least tamed it. Then move on to work on others.

Successful life and time management is a journey not a destination. As in any journey, the starting point is just as important as the destination.

**One tip**: don't try to deal with them all at once. Select the most important ones and work on them until you've beaten them. Then confidently tackle the next ones on your list. It may take some time, but, if you focus your energies, **you can take control!**

*PRO-TIP:* When you deliver a speech, would you like to be in such 'flow' that your words come naturally, and your gestures **become one with the spoken message?** It's all in how you use your mind, imagination, and focus. Before you speak, mentally visualize your audience with love and with an eager expectation to give them the gift of your message, 'seeing' their receptive faces, 'hearing' their positive responses, and 'feeling' the power of your words as they roll out just the way you had planned. Be so immersed in the moment that your focus is on your message and your audience. Your gestures and movement will become one with your words, and you will discover the joy of connecting with your audience with the power of the spoken word.

© *Dilip R. Abayasekara, Accredited Speaker and Past Toastmasters International President* www.drdilip.com

# Converting Filler Time to Foundation Time
*How to re-create or liberate 365 hours each year*

**How would you like to re-create or liberate a minimum of 365 hours each year?** That is the equivalent of over 9 weeks of time. Very simple process: reclaim, repurpose, or convert a minimum of one hour each day.

One of the important secrets to regaining control of your time and life is in the conversion of 'filler' or wasted time into 'foundation' or constructive time. Recapturing or re-creating those seemingly 'insignificant' slivers of time (5 - 15-minute chunks) and converting them to more constructive use will make a major difference in your life, leadership, and career advancement.

I'd like to suggest these ideas that might help you do just that - capture those 'insignificant' minutes and convert them to useful time. Each of them will help you free up an average of 5 minutes, some substantially more.

**Simply incorporate 12 or more of them of them into each day and free up or re-create a minimum of one hour for more useful time.**

- Useful time that builds success foundations under your dreams and goals.
- Useful time that leads you productively in the direction you've laid out for your future.
- Useful time that previously was thrown away.
- Useful time that allows you to invest time in building and maintaining important relationships.

## At home
- Bunch or group your errands
- Spend 5 minutes each day pre-planning your schedule and activities.
- Trade off with neighbours or friends and share common chores - i.e., kids to school
- Use your time in the shower as pre-planning time to mentally go over your daily schedule and goals
- Coordinate your business clothing to include suits, shirts, ties, and accessories before bedtime
- Never make more than one trip if possible. Don't backtrack!
- Use a voice mail system on your phone. Some systems assign voice mailboxes for each family member
- Open your personal mail over a recycling bin

- Multi-task to combine activities that would normally demand down time or waiting time, for example, cooking and laundry or menu planning
- Agree on a special family time to discuss and plan family activities

## At work

- Spend 5 minutes each day reviewing the current day and pre-planning activities and goals for the next day. Revise your schedule based on 4 P's of Personal Performance principles (see page 62).
- Keep a folder with required reading close at hand for those 'on-hold' times
- Keep career advancement e-books on your e-reader, computer, and smart phone for creative fill-ins
- Keep a career enhancement book close at hand for reading breaks
- Open your mail over your wastebasket or recycle bin
- Batch your phone calls for specific times each day
- Return phone calls at specific times each day
- Check your email only at specific times each day and return emails then
- Keep your internet use to a minimum and focus on work during work
- Do internet surfing, Facebook, LinkedIn, Twitter posts, etc. ONLY on your breaks and resist the temptation to check it during work time
- Plan what you are going to say before you make a call and have the relevant information or files available for quick reference
- Multi-task to do more than one job, alternating back and forth between activities instead of just waiting for something to warm up, print, or load
- Trade off with co-workers to create some 'uninterrupted' planning and creative time
- Take a few minutes before you leave to de-clutter your desk
- Take a few minutes before you leave to put out important items for attention first thing in the morning

## While waiting

- Carry a book/e-reader/tablet or something to read with you
- Use your cell phone to retrieve and return messages
- Use your smart phone to check your email or make post to social media
- Have a mini-recorder to dictate letters or brainstorm ideas. Use your smart phone for this function
- Check your various lists and update your action items
- Check your schedule and revise, as needed

- Brainstorm solutions to challenges you have with your business or personal life

## While commuting

- Turn your car into a mobile university - listen to MP3s or CDs en-route
- If using public systems - use a personal MP3 player with earphones
- Use your smart phone or GPS to help plan your route
- Use your smart phone to locate addresses and directions for places you need to find
- Spend the time revising your schedule and revisiting your priorities and goals
- Spend the time rehearsing your presentation or sales pitch

## While traveling

- Pre-select your seat when possible. Most airlines will still allow you to do this in advance of coming to airport
- Check in on-line and print your boarding pass. Then go right to security and your gate to save time
- Pack selected coordinates to allow yourself to take less with you on trips
- Use a packing list to ensure you have everything you need. Print it and put it in your bag along with your home and local contact information
- Pack and travel light to avoid long check-ins and waiting for your baggage at your destination
- Carry selected reading/e-reader to review en-route
- Load your smart phone with e-books – like this one!
- Take along postcards or send notes and thank you 's to selected friends, customers, suppliers, and other important people in your life. Take along stamps and drop them in the nearest post box on arrival
- Take time to review and plan your week in relation to **4P's of Personal Performance.** (see page 62)
- Take the time to specifically plan and revise your planning tool
- Review magazines and articles that apply to your field of study
- When driving away from home, use your smart phone or GPS to help plan your route. *I've found Google Maps helpful around the globe.*
- Use your smart phone to locate places you need to find.

I realize the above are not the 'end all - be all' of how to recapture your time. The exercise here was to show you a few examples of areas where you could reclaim a few minutes here and there to free up time for better or more productive use. You can easily free up an **hour-a-day** if you focus!

As you become more focused and proficient in recapturing and reclaiming your time, you'll become aware of a multitude of ideas and activities that you can use to convert your filler time into foundation time. Don't despise those 'insignificant' minutes. Just like the 'secret' of compound interest, those minutes if captured and reinvested in your career or future will *multiply* and pay fabulous dividends.

If you come up with some unique or creative ideas, would you, please email me and share them? If included in subsequent versions of this work, we will credit you and send you a copy of the updated version for your own use. You can email me at: bob@ideaman.net

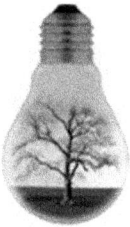

## Tap into the power of your health

Investing time to ensure you are in good health is important to successfully tackle the demands and pressures in this increasingly hectic world. Keeping your energy levels and mental well being on track is a worthy investment.

- **Manage your stress and anxiety** by doing some form of exercise: for example, run, swim, ride, ski, jog, tennis, or dance.
- **Create a healthy diet** that gives you the energy needed to succeed.
- **Get annual check-ups** – enlist your doctor as a part of your team.
- **Drink water** – keep your body and your brain hydrated. Water also helps flush toxins and other 'junk' out of your system.
- **Sleep is a weapon** – sleep more; sleep better so you have the energy to get more done. Don't watch the news before bedtime.
- **Take naps when your energy is low.** Learn from successful people like Einstein who understood the value of listening to his body and allowing time to recharge.
- **Plan well in advance to reduce stress**. For example, lay out your clothes the night before so you don't have to rush in the morning.

# Communication skills

## Five Steps to persuasion
### ...ideas to create successful presentations

Every presentation aims to persuade an audience. We seek to persuade them to listen and perhaps agree with the viewpoints we present. Crafting our thoughts and ideas is what proves our professionalism.

- **Get their attention:** If you don't capture my attention, you'll never gain my acceptance or my action on your behalf. What does it take to do that? Do it!
- **Demonstrate their need to know:** This is where you help me see the relevance of what you are about to share. If I don't see a need in my life, career, or company I will not respond favourably to your call to action and you are wasting time for us both.
- **Satisfy that need:** This is where you outline the solutions in ways that I can apply and benefit.
- **Visualize the results:** Help me see the *finished* results, the changes as outlined in your solution. Give me a *mental* picture of my need being met and my satisfaction attained, and I will be more receptive to act or buy.

- **Request their action:** This is where many mediocre sales people blow it. **Ask for the order.** Call me to action! Challenge me to do something great!

This is a summary of the steps behind persuasion. Keep them in mind as you structure your presentation. Keep in mind what the audience reaction will be to each area. Selling your ideas as a presenter is very like what professional salespeople do with their clients and the process follows a similar path.

# Moving upward

*"the top predictor of success and upward mobility, professionally, is how much you enjoy public speaking and how effective you are at it!"*

**Stanford University Survey for AT&T**

*"As soon as you move one step up from the bottom, your effectiveness depends on your ability to reach others through the spoken or written word."*

**Peter Drucker - Author**

*"Effective speaking skills are an essential foundation for success in any endeavor. Professionally or personally, it is one of the most important skills you'll ever acquire! And it is easily acquired!"*

**Bob 'idea Man' Hooey**
**Accredited Speaker**
**Presentations Skills Success Coach**

# Where do I stand now in my journey as a presenter?

Think about the last time you gave a presentation or spoke in front of a group (*however small*). Think back and give yourself some honest feedback on your performance and perceptions as a speaker or presenter. The key to a successful journey or goal is in accurately determining your starting point.

Someone asked me these types of questions at the start of my Toastmasters journey in 1991. I admit I said "NO" to too many of them at that time. Each, however, points to a skill that can be easily acquired, polished, and applied. **Remember** these questions are for your information only, so be honest in your self-assessment.

## DO I PRESENTLY...

| | Yes | No |
|---|---|---|
| 1. Feel comfortable talking to other people? | ___ | ___ |
| 2. Have trouble explaining my views or ideas? | ___ | ___ |
| 3. Have nervous habits when I speak, such as saying um, uh Ok, you know, and ah, or fumbling with buttons, clothes, glasses, or change in my pocket? | ___ | ___ |
| 4. Focus on the audience's needs and interests when I make a presentation? (It's not about me) | ___ | ___ |
| 5. Plan presentations with a clear purpose in mind? | ___ | ___ |
| 6. Appear natural and sincere when I'm speaking? | ___ | ___ |
| 7. Listen carefully and analytically to other speakers? | ___ | ___ |
| 8. Feel comfortable receiving feedback from others? | ___ | ___ |
| 9. Offer feedback in a constructive, positive way that doesn't cause others pain or embarrassment? | ___ | ___ |

Your answers to these questions may prove to be the guideposts to the specific areas that you need to learn and the skills you need to apply in your pursuit to become a powerful presenter. It might be a good idea to come back several times as you proceed through this course of study and evaluate your progress.

# Three key ideas to 'successful' presentations (speeches)

In public speaking, the cardinal rule to being truly effective is **"NEVER BE BORING!"** But how do we do this when we are nervous and under *pressure to perform?*

I've been teaching my clients and various classes that the "three key ideas to speaking success" are based on acquiring the knowledge you need to successfully capture their attention, to connect with your audience, and to achieve your shared objectives.

**Those three key ideas to speaking success are:**

**KNOW** your subject or topic
**KNOW** your audience
**KNOW** yourself

**If you know your subject** and are thoroughly prepared, you will be much more relaxed and effective than if you are 'winging' it.

Taking time to organize and delve into your topic will give you a sense of the depth you bring to the platform. It will also give you much more information than you will be able to deliver, which gives you back-up information for additional presentations and questions. This confidence, based on acquired knowledge, works wonders in helping to keep the "butterflies flying in formation," as we used to say in **Toastmasters**.

**If you know your audience**, you will be better prepared to effectively analyze their needs and select from the body of knowledge you've acquired on your topic to serve or solve those needs; to present something that is relevant and helpful to them.

The better you know or *understand* their backgrounds, history, connections, education, gender, and their ages; the better you will be able to construct and deliver your presentation in a way that is interesting, relevant, and informative to them.

**If you know yourself**, you can draw on your own experiences and build on your own strengths in developing your own speaking style. You can share your own ideas and 'unique' stories in a way that allows you to be most effective. Self-knowledge is a tool of effective and successful communication.

Continually ask yourself, *"If I was in the audience, why would I be interested in this point or topic?"* Then simply make sure you have a good answer for that question. Your audiences are people, just like you. The better you know yourself, the better equipped you are to effectively reach them.

By skilfully combining your knowledge of self, your subject, and your audience, you will effectively increase your impact. You will also expand your impact as a presenter, interviewee, or speaker.

## A final note here:

Be sure to apply the 3 P's of public speaking –
**PREPARATION, PRACTICE, and PERFORMANCE!**

There is no substitute for being prepared, by practicing until you are certain that you are ready to present your material in a confident manner. Anyone who says they just get up and *fake it* is leading you down the wrong path. Prepare, practice, and polish and, then, confidently walk on stage and *play* with the audience. That is what I have learned to do, and it works well for me.

The masters *only* make it look easy. They have put in the time, (lots of it) far from the public eye, long before they are introduced… and it shows!

## Ideas to 'handle' your nervousness about speaking

Here are a few easily applied ideas and techniques on how to handle and overcome your nervousness:

1.  **Don't fight it!** Realize that being a *little* nervous is normal. I accept that and allow that nervous energy to propel me to a more impactful presentation.

2.  Being **mentally prepared** is a good part of winning and Speaking for Success. Visualize your confidence in front of the audience.

3.  **Do something physical to work out the nervous energy**. Being physically prepared is an important aspect of the journey and can help you in controlling nerves and being mentally prepared.
    *   Take a brisk walk.
    *   Don't sit with your legs or arms crossed.
    *   Let your arms dangle at your sides while you're sitting waiting to speak.

- While your arms are dangling, twirl your wrists so your fingers shake loosely.
- Pretend you're wearing a heavy overcoat or jacket and feel it on your shoulders as your shrug them up and down.
- Waggle your jaw back and forth a few times to loosen it up. This relaxes your face and allows you to speak better and be heard.
- Deep breathing can help, but don't hyperventilate.
- Use the power of self-talk, say, 'Let's go!' or use some of the affirmations I share with you later in this Speaking for Success manual.

**Don't be self-conscious** about having a warmup routine. Champion athletes and high achievers do warm ups because they know it helps them prepare to do their best. It reduces the chance of injury. Warming up allows you to be at your best in front of an audience. It allows you to loosen up and be more relaxed. Find out what works for you and build it into your preparation routine.

**Here is a mental tip:** Nervousness and *'being excited'* are two sides of the same equation. Mentally move into the *'being excited'* about the opportunity where you share your ideas and to positively influence this audience's lives for the better!

**PRO-TIP:** The difference between the good speakers and the awesome speakers is usually not in the speaking itself. It's in their ability to reach their audience at a level that improves something about their lives so that they, in some way, become more than they were when they first sat down.
© **Steve Lowell**, *CSP* www.stevelowell.com

# Bob's Foundations for Speaking Success!

When this material is taught in person, one of the areas covered as an overview is what I call **'Foundations for Speaking Success!'**

Investing time to make sure you have completely thought through and answered these questions is essential to your confidence and success on the platform. These ideas were gleaned from conversations with fellow professional speakers. I've added to their wisdom from my own first-hand experience. These *'foundations'* have worked for me, and **they will work for you!** The knowledge gleaned from their *wisdom* is the secret to being able to walk confidently up to the front and deliver a message that means something to your audiences.

**The secret** to ensure the audience gets the best presentation possible, with the most value, blended with personal stories and teaching points, **is in the pre-preparation**. This is what you do *well* before you start crafting your presentation.

**Questions,** thoughtful questions like these, can be the keys that unlock the door to success in any venture. This is no less true if your desire is to be a confident, powerful speaker, who connects with their audience, and leaves them wanting more.

- **WHY** are you speaking? (What is your expertise or purpose?)

- **WHAT** do you want to accomplish? (Be clear!)

- **WHO** is your audience? (What do they know or need to know?)

- **WHEN** will you be speaking? (Time of day, position on program?)

- **HOW** long will you be speaking? (Structure accordingly.)

- **WHERE** will you be speaking? (Room, geographical location)

- **WHAT** tools will you use? (Choose them wisely.)

Doing your homework in preparing yourself, your research, and your presentation is the secret behind your success in any endeavor. Prepare Yourself to WIN!

# Mastery of the message
## *Using the 3 M's of Speaking Success*

*I still remember the first experience of being in the 'magic of the moment.' We'd truly connected – my audience and me. They were with me fully, completely. I could take them where I wanted. WOW, what an experience! It was amazing, and nearly 30 years later, I can still vividly recall being in the moment (zone) with them and how it felt. Awesome!*

Yes, I have been there since, and work to go there often, but the freshness of that first experience lives on in my memory. It inspires and drives me to work diligently to prepare each session, to give my best, and to be fully there for my audiences.

**That is the true 'mastery of the message' – as shown in the results and reactions of those who receive and act on it!**

Mastery is an attainable skill; if you care enough and are willing to pay the price and put in the effort. I have carefully observed my CAPS, NSA, and GSF colleagues and speaker friends. I have watched those who are acknowledged *masters* on the platform and in the training room, to see what they do and what they bring to their mastery. Each has their own unique style and substance. Each has a shared commitment to mastery and serving their audience's highest needs. I have sought to apply what I observed in my own time in front of audiences.

So, let's explore the **3 M's of Speaking Success**™ that lead to the mastery of the message and give you entrance into the magic of the shared moment.

## Message

**First, make sure you have something to say!** This should be a given, but it isn't to many emerging speakers. All too often, I have seen beginning speakers who simply *parrot* something they've read or heard from another speaker or author. It is not real in their lives or *relevant* for them or for their audiences and sadly, it shows.

Not that sharing a message *gleaned* from a master or a group of masters is a bad thing. Presenting it as though it is your own is! It is unprofessional and borders on plagiarism or intellectual property theft. **DON'T DO IT!** Make sure you've *fully* researched and 'thought' through your material, so you have some depth and are not just another 'book-report' speaker.

To reach your audience you need to *filter your message* through your life and your experiences to make sure it is real and relevant to them. If it is not real or relevant to you, it won't connect, and you'll fail.

- How well do you know your audience? What do you know about them that would guide you in the research and the crafting of your message?
- How much time have they given you to share it?
- What gems of wisdom, what stories, what experiences can you draw on to flesh it out and make your message live, connect, and remain embedded in their hearts?
- What do you want them to learn, understand, or act on from your message?

Dig deep in your message and prepare it well.

**The masters never shirk their diligence in preparation!**

## Messenger

**You as the messenger bear a strong responsibility for the success of your message being received and acted upon by your audiences.**

It needs to be fully integrated and involved in your life to become real and relevant to them. It needs to be in line with what you truly believe to be credible and even more importantly, achievable by action on their part.

**They will believe your message and act on it, when they believe you!**
What is your motive and motivation for speaking to them? It is important to know why you are speaking and where you are coming from, if you would seek to succeed with them, connect with them, and impact their lives.

Be honest with yourself in what you seek here. Do you seek to simply entertain yourself at their expense or use them for therapy? Or, are you seeking to impart and inspire them to gain knowledge, act, and rally around the flag to a better life or a more effective career or business?

**The masters know themselves and share openly and boldly!**

Knowing yourself helps you take what you know about them and apply it in crafting your message and in more skilfully delivering it.

80

# Method

This is the *easier* part of the presentation equation. ☺ If you've dug deep enough to make sure what you must say is truly valuable and has relevance to your audience, made sure it is in-line with your own integrity and life; it will be so much easier to communicate effectively to an audience.

Once you've decided what outcome you desire from the communication of your message, it is easier to structure the delivery system. Depending on the message and the desired outcome, *(and of course the time constraints of the time you must deliver it)*, you can blend in stories, audience interaction and exercises, and inspirational bits.

**Time is one of the biggest factors that impact the delivery method you chose.**

*I've grown to love the interaction with audiences. I find when keynoting, that my ability to incorporate active dialogue with them is more challenging than during breakouts and training sessions. I still work in some areas where they can actively feedback or respond to the message being shared.*

Asking questions, getting them to share something with a neighbour, or simply using rhetorical questions to draw them in; these techniques will work in building a bridge to the hearts and minds of your audiences.

The effective use of storytelling is *under-rated* and ignored by speakers in many levels and arenas. Sometimes the most effective way to communicate a message is to wrap it tenderly in a story. How many Sunday school lessons do you still remember; how many nursery rhymes or children's stories can you still recall? My bet, lots of them – and if you can recall the story, you can retain the lesson and the message behind the story.

The masters weave stories to last a lifetime!

## A few final ideas...

If you want to achieve the 'mastery of the message' you will need to dig deep to master yourself first and then draw from that in preparing and delivering your message. **Applying the 3 M's will help you succeed.**

You owe it to your audiences to diligently prepare and to bring forth your best. Anything else would be a waste of everyone's time and energy.

**Seeking to become a *'master of the message'* is the beginning of attaining the mastery – and the journey is worth it!**

*One question I frequently get from my clients and students is **"How do you give your presentations without notes?"** A good question! Sometimes I do use notes. I don't have a problem with having someone using them, if they are unobtrusive and don't take audience focus away from your presentation.*

There are several famous speakers who effectively use notes in their presentations. Using notes as a back-up to give you a sense of confidence is okay. So is using notes as reference or to quote a fact or quotation. Keep them simple and don't get in the habit of depending on them or obviously refer to them during your presentation.

One exercise shared with my students was to ask them to hold up and look at their hand. **"What do you see?"** They usually say, "A thumb and four fingers," which is of course, the obvious answer.

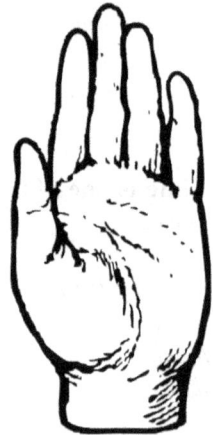

My answer to that same question is *"A presentation, without notes, up to 20 minutes."* I see an opening, three points and a conclusion.

**I can remember 5 points or 5 things! Can't you?**

When we keep it simple and focus on the main points, it makes it easier to remember.

**PRO-TIP:** Business involves courageous dialogue… the conversations that matter most and are mostly avoided. Taking time to address issues, provide feedback and resolve conflict early on. This will build a healthy team, happy clients, and save you time and energy that you can redirect into building your business.
© *Charmaine Hammond & Rebecca Kirstein* www.raiseadream.com

**PRO-TIP:** What you do and think 5 minutes before any presentation … will make or break it. **Would you like to connect deeper with your audience/team every time you present?**

**Here's the problem.** Most people spend hours and hours preparing their presentation and rarely take the time to prepare their mindset just before it's show time. This is true whether you have a presentation, a one-on-one sales call, or even an interview. **It can be even worse!** Have you ever given a presentation where you just didn't feel connected? Many speakers blame it on the audience, but the reality is most of the time a speaker needs to look in the mirror if he or she didn't connect with the audience. **What can you do? The answer is quite simple!**

In 2001, I won the World Championship of Public Speaking. Though I had rehearsed and practiced tirelessly for over two months on one speech, one of the most important things I did was pull out my pocket questions just before I took the stage. To this day I ask the *same questions* before taking the stage. Creating the connection is crucial whether it is a high-paid keynote speech or working on a new story at my own Toastmaster club.

The moment you take the stage, **your 'mindset' is everything**. You don't have to be perfect. You don't have to be the ultimate expert. The audience will forgive almost any mistake, but they won't forgive you if you're not there for them. I ask myself *Four Crucial Questions* before taking the stage to ensure I **connect** with them.

Remember: **"Skill set, without mindset, will leave your audience upset."** Speakers who connect deeper with their audience will get more laughs, get referred more often, and simply have more fun every time!

**What are these powerful questions?** What is my intent? Am I present? Will I have fun? How would I give this presentation if I knew it was my 'last' one ever? These will ground you and keep you present. The audience will forgive minor mistakes and some major. The one mistake they will not forgive is, if you are there for your ego rather than their insight. When people who compete in contests are there for the trophy, the audience can clearly sense it.
© *Darren Lacroix, CSP, Accredited Speaker* www.darrenlacroix.com
www.theconnectcard.com

# Toastmasters - Accredited Speaker Program

*Over the past 20 years, people have inquired about my Professional Level Accredited Speaker Designation (Toastmasters International) and how it came to be. As it played a critical part in fueling my desire to become a professional speaker and in preparation of doing so, I include this brief story of my journey for your information and perhaps encouragement.*

In November of 1993, 32 Toastmasters from around the world sent in audition tapes and applications for judging in the first level of the Toastmasters International prestigious professional level Accredited Speaker Program. (Update 2023: Only 90 now including 12 Canadians)

In February of 1994, *only five* were notified of acceptance and invited to speak at the Toastmasters International convention for second level judging. Of those five, three were Canadians. All three were from BC, from the same Toastmasters Club – ASK, the Advanced Speaker Klub. They were DTMs, **Margaret Hope, Judy Johnson and me.**

**How did this unique result happen?**

It started back in 1993, when seven BC Toastmasters met to investigate the Toastmasters International Accredited Speaker program and continued to meet monthly for the next year and a bit. Each month we would meet, present, and evaluate our results. We worked as a team in all respects including creating a non-Toastmasters event where we each presented and recorded our presentations. We did that twice, so we could choose the better of the two recordings. In November of 1994, Margaret Hope, Judy Johnson, and I felt ready to apply and sent in our audition tapes.

Margaret received her Accredited Speaker designation in San Diego in 1995, becoming the 41st speaker inducted into Toastmasters Hall of Fame for this award. Judy and I were not successful in our first attempt in San Diego. I spoke again the following year in St. Louis and was not successful. I took 1997 off as I had taken on the District Governor role for BC's 4500 Toastmasters. But I kept working on it to hone my skills.

I moved into the realm of professional speaking taking my presentations to a new level. I helped launch CAPS Vancouver in April of 1997 as a part of founding CAPS National across Canada.

*The dream became a reality when I walked across a stage to the cheers of 2000-plus, fellow Toastmasters from around the world to be inducted into the Toastmasters Hall of Fame and received mine in Palm Desert in 1998; becoming the 48-professional level Accredited Speaker in our history, and only the 5th Canadian to earn this designation.*

Toastmasters initiated their coveted professional level, Accredited Speakers program in 1981, some 37 years ago to recognize those members for their **"professionalism and outstanding achievements in public speaking"**.

*I focused on this program early in my Toastmasters life, as my dream was to become a professional speaker. I remember when I got my Able Toastmaster (ATM); it came with a flyer for the Accredited Speaker Program which said in big letters,* **"Are you good enough to be a PRO?"** *I wrote on it,* **"Not yet, but I will be!"** *For two years it challenged me from the wall above my desk!*

www.toastmasters.org/membership/accredited-speakerfor more information on the professional level program and its Hall of Fame recipients.

The real 'win' in this program, wasn't the designation itself or the worldwide recognition, although that was very satisfying. **The *real win* for me was in the progression of my skills and entry into the world of professional speaking;** in being able to have people see, first hand, the value in what I brought to the training room or the platform and pay me accordingly. The real win was in being better at sharing my messages for the benefit of my audiences around the world.

Over the years, many of us (AS) have been offering mentorship to fellow Toastmasters. In 2017, we saw that multiplied when 6 speakers joined our ranks as Accredited Speakers in Vancouver, BC. **We now number 90.** (**Editor's note**: *Toastmasters did a profile on Bob for the Jan. 2018 issue of **The Toastmaster** magazine.*)

# Sales and customer service success skills

## A few thoughts on setting sales success goals, 'even' in tough times

Ultimately, **the *measurement and review of your value*** to your firm, as a salesperson, **is directly tied to your ability to sell.** Your leadership team will look at your sales volume at any time during your firm's term of measurement. That look might be monthly, quarterly, a twice-yearly performance appraisal, or year end. But it will happen, and it makes good sense to be both aware of it and prepare to ensure your sales results *stand up* under this scrutiny.

You may be providing intrinsic value to your team and your firm by your activities. However, when all is said and done, your sales results are the primary factor used to evaluate your performance and promotion. That is the harsh truth.

Sales master **W. Clement Stone** challenged his sales team to ***"Set a goal so big, that if you achieved it, it would blow your mind."***

**This is not a time to play it safe**, nor is it time to listen to those (even those who may be relatively successful in selling) who would tell you setting goals is a waste of time. It isn't and your success and growth in the sales field will be directly tied to your ability to formally set and achieve your goals. Set a realistic goal that will push you; one that will stretch you in its achievement. **Set a goal worthy of your potential** and then work diligently to achieve it.

In sales, life, and business, we have proven results and thousands of stories of people who formally set goals who went on to substantially greater success than their counterparts. You can too, if you *"plan and then work your plan."* You know that this investment of your time in setting your goals for the year, and revisiting and revising them as needed, provides the roadmap for your sales success, *'more so'* in tough times when every sale counts.

**Take a few minutes and go through a brief planning process considering your BIG Goal.**

Depending on your focus (Sales, commission, units) here is how you might do it.

Set your income or sales target (choose which works best for you) or,

Set your commission and/or bonus target (if this works better for you) or,

Divide your yearly target (#1) by the average commission and/or bonus per sale (#2). If you need help, go back over your previous year or talk to your sales manager. This calculation should yield an annual 'unit' sales target needed to reach your sales target, income, or commission.

You can then divide this number (either #1, #2, #3) by 12 to give your monthly target, or divide it by 50 (average number of weeks with 2 weeks of holidays or 48 if you take 4 weeks) to get your weekly number.

### See it! Write it! Achieve it!

However, you work it out, it is a good idea to break your 'BIG' sales goal into measurable weekly and/or monthly results.

That makes it easier to track your success and make changes if you notice you need to bump it up to keep on track.

### Now what?

What is next if you are serious about meeting this BIG goal?

What activities (average) do you need to be involved in on a weekly or monthly basis to reach your calculated results?

How many outbound sales calls do you need to make to explore or set up an initial sales interview?

How many (average) sales interviews or demonstrations (daily, weekly, monthly, quarterly) do you need to qualify a customer where an order can be placed, or a proposal created?

How many (average) proposals or contracts need to be delivered daily (weekly, monthly, and quarterly) to close the deal?

If needed, you can go back over your last year's results (keep in mind you are setting a big goal that will s-t-r-e-t-c-h you) to get a sense of what is needed to get to the sale. When you have worked out your sales numbers in relation to your BIG sales goal, then you are ready. Being prepared is one of the *secrets* to being successful in sales.

**Henry Ford** said, ***"Before everything else, being ready is the Secret of Success!"***

Keep these numbers close to you as a reference guide to chart your progress. Measure them frequently and honestly and decide where you need help. Ask for help when you need it.

Do you need help with prospecting or qualifying?
Do you need help demonstrating your firm's products or explaining your firm's services, policies, etc.?
Do you need help with closing?
Do you need help in follow up to create additional sales and repeat business?

As you go through this process it may become apparent that you need to invest in your own development as a selling professional. That is good! Over the centuries, our top sales leaders were people who realized the importance of investing in their future success, today! Their preparation allowed them to productively weather economic upheavals, storms, and tough times.

**Johann Friedrich von Schiller** wrote, ***"The average estimate themselves by what they do, the above average by what they are."***

# One percent better!

*"Excellence results from doing 100 things 1 percent better, rather than one thing 100 percent better."* **Author Unknown**

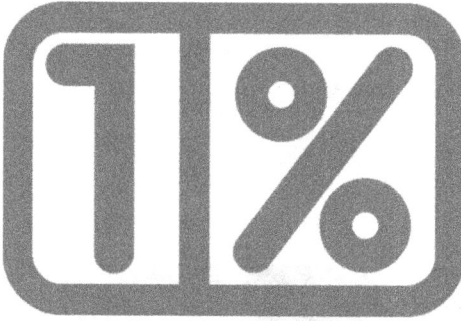

One of the biggest obstacles to growth is the 'misguided' quest for the big idea, the big break, the big sale, or the big change. Success, sales, and growth happen one step at a time, one improvement at a time, and often a simple, one-percent-at-a-time.

Sure, there are many stories of major breakthroughs and advances; perhaps you've even experienced one or more yourself. However, when you look at what led up to them, you'll often see multiple efforts to improve, research, prepare, and experiment. *This is often the case in my life and business as I work and prepare in advance of the successful completion or creative breakthrough.*

It would be so easy, if we could simply wait until the ***big million-dollar idea*** drops into our brains or laps and then simply reap the benefits. It would also be *unrealistic* to live that way. It would be like buying a lotto ticket as a means of paying your monthly bills. Top performers and leaders are never fully satisfied with where they or their teams are.

They have what many would call 'creative discontent' in that they can always see ways of tweaking or making it better. Many of the ones I meet or work with live this way.

**Peters and Waterman (In Search of Excellence)** wrote, *"The essence of excellence is the thousand concrete, minute-to-minute actions performed by everyone in an organization to keep a company on its course."*

**Sam Walton** of Wal-Mart fame was famous for looking at his competition with the eye of learning 'one thing' he could use to make what he and his team did a bit better. Sam Walton built a large, successful, multi-national company from a very little one by applying this concept of continuous improvement.

**Jack Welsh** made some amazing and profitable changes in GE by essentially doing the same thing.

- **What are your competitors doing better that you can apply?**

- **Are there 10 to 15 specific areas where you can make changes that will give you a 1% improvement?**

- **Write the ideas for improvement down and schedule specific time to make them happen.**

**One percent better** can be your rallying call in the pursuit of excellence and success in your leadership, career, or company. Create and then change!

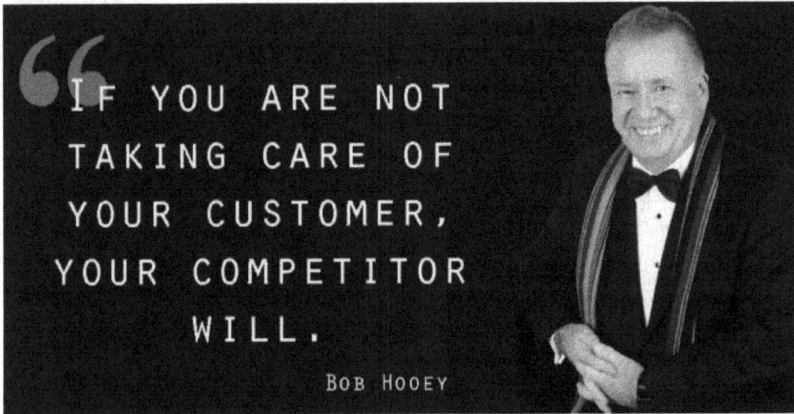

"IF YOU ARE NOT TAKING CARE OF YOUR CUSTOMER, YOUR COMPETITOR WILL.

BOB HOOEY

*Interesting how this quotation has grown legs. It has shown up in an Inc. article on the top 10 quotes for salespeople (#9), on Brian Tracy's 101 best quotes (#2), and even on a training wall in South Africa. It works!*

**PRO-TIP:** Most people think you're selling to the person in front of you. You're not. The person you're really selling to is WHO THAT PERSON IMAGINES THEMSELVES TO BE.

So, you need to speak to their inner rock star, successful entrepreneur, writer, farmer, environmentalist, musician, race car driver…the person who is really driving the bus of their buying decisions. And that only happens when you focus on what they will feel & experience after using your product/service. So there. 😊

© *Kim Duke* www.salesdivas.com

# Dedicated to our 'Clients', who may choose, at times, to be our 'Customers'

As you delve into this section on enhanced **'Sales Success'** you might notice we have used the word 'client' here and there, in some cases using both 'client/customer'. This is a deliberate choice in our vocabulary and a foundational change in mindset we feel necessary to help you enhance your chances of attracting and retaining customers who will become your biggest fans and champions (clients). This will result in allowing you to Generate More Sales and sustained growth and profit.

Business success (whether retail, service-based, or even direct buyer connections) is built on establishing mutually profitable relationships; relationships where you make the customer (client) feel special.

**When you *'Make ME Feel Special!'* you enhance your chances of converting me from a one-time customer to a long-term raving client.** *(Excerpt from the book with the same name – invest in the book for your success)*

## Client vs. Customer: Aren't they really the same thing?

**Webster's defines these two seemingly interchangeable words**

**Customer:** one that purchases a 'commodity' or service

**Client:** one that is **'under-the-protection'** of another; a person who engages the professional advice or services of another

Ever wondered why the top performing business owners and sales superstars sell so much better and make so much more money than their counterparts? Plus, they seem to do it so much easier too. Their secret is in how they 'visualize' and more effectively approach everyone, which results in such higher levels of success with their prospective clients.

**They see clients** vs. customers walk into their locations and act accordingly.

**They see clients** when they pick up the phone or walk into an office or boardroom.

**They see clients** when there is a concern or something that needs to be fixed or replaced and they act with a long-term view.

**They see clients** who become raving fans and champions for them.

Take a moment and reflect on the underlying 'differences' in the meanings of these two words. The way a person, who does business with you, can be approached and treated will directly impact your results. In the past, you may have referred to them as customers. Please think of them as clients!

When I started writing our successful on-line **'*Secret Selling Tips*'** series (2006), we called them 'customers' to align with the typical retail terminology used by our first client. We transitioned back to 'Clients' with an explanation of our thinking in year two to help them profitably 'change' their viewpoint and culture.

Prior to creating and launching '*Secret Selling Tips*' I had thought of them (customers) as clients. This focus was, in part, from the many years of serving my design clients who came to me for help in creating the kitchen, bathroom, or other room of their dreams. This view was reinforced from connections with leading selling professionals and top performing business owners and managers across North America who shared this mindset.

Perhaps it would be a 'profitable' idea for you to follow their lead. The key to this mental shift lies in understanding what **'under the protection'** of another means in your client (customer) interactions.

**My thought:** This means you don't 'simply' sell someone a service or product 'just' to ensure you make the largest short-term profit or commission possible.

You **'serve them best'** by helping them fully explore their options to make the 'best choice' when they purchase something or engage a service from you!

You **'serve them best'** by working with them to purchase something that serves their needs from you. We all need to 'sell' to stay in business and this focus is an important part of the sales/customer service process.

Even if they are not able to clearly articulate what results, products, or services they need; it is important that you, as a top performing professional, work to understand and appreciate exactly what your clients need when they do business with you and your company. The better you do that, the more you will succeed over the long-term. This service or protection mentality also builds solid repeat sales and referral business for you.

When you determine what outcome or benefit is needed (solid qualifying skills), you can gently lead or guide them to that successful outcome. You become their solutions provider as well as their trusted guide. When you do, you become a 'high trust' professional advisor/advocate who protects them.

This earned trust builds a foundation for them to remain your client for life and to become your biggest fan. It also builds a foundation for a long-term valuable client friendship. It also allows you to be a productive salesperson.

In our online sales success and print publications we've shared that research shows people 'still' do business with those they trust and like. **That research remains true in 2018.** Keep that in mind as you engage with potential clients as you move forward after reading this book.

One of the secrets to business and/or selling success is **to 'maximize' each client relationship** by ensuring you demonstrate your 'genuine' commitment to helping them, not just selling them. That mental shift is reinforced when you think of them as 'valued' clients not 'just' customers. The result is they will buy from you again and encourage their friends and contacts to follow their lead in selecting you to serve them. People love to 'buy' but hate being 'sold'.

*"To satisfy our customers' needs, we'll give them what they want, not what we want to give them."*
**Steve James**

# Building a successful career in selling or business

When all is said and done, there are essentially **THREE productive ways to increase your selling results and/or build your business:**

Increase the **number of clients** you attract and retain to deal with you.

Increase the **average size of the sale** for each client.

Increase the frequency or **number of times** each client returns and buys.

**Hint:** Look for ways to attract more clients in the services and product mix you offer.

Condition your mind to look for break-through ideas and creative solutions. Investigate other industries, look at their success stories and best practices and see if they hold a secret that you can transfer to yours. (i.e. Fed-Ex simply adapted the central distribution system used by the banking system for courier delivery. Fred did ok with this transplanted break-through!) Jack Welsh of GE did this as did Sam Walton of Wal-Mart fame.

**Jay Abraham says,** *"Break throughs let you outthink, out leverage, out market, out sell, out impact, out defend, out maneuver, and continuously outwit your competition at every level."*

Jay suggests we should look for break through or transferable ideas in marketing, innovation, creative, operations, sourcing, technology, systems, process, selling, financing, product mix, service list, and distribution.

**How about looking for ways to add-on or cross-sell?**

**Adding on** helps move the client to a larger or superior product, package, or service. It is based on really *'understanding'* the intended use and realizing the basic product or service will fail to meet the real needs of your client. If so, you are doing the client a disservice by allowing them to buy something that will not meet their needs. Additionally, you are building in a possible unsatisfied result, which will adversely impact your repeat sales potential. The selling professional works with their client to ensure they get what they need and that it satisfies them.

94

**Cross selling** introduces your client to additional products or service. Offer them alternatives that perform better and are in their best interest. Telus, Rogers, Bell, Fido, and AT&T do this well with bundling: Voice mail, call waiting, auto call back, 2nd line, autodial, caller ID, 3rd line for security, 4th line for fax, cable and computer information delivery systems. Some companies have affiliates or special warranty or insurance programs.

**Test market your offerings, product mix and services offered.**
Experiment with your Website, advertising, promotional materials, selling and direct mail letters, live sales presentations and in-store demos, guarantees, USP's, pricing points, volume purchase and discounts, or financing.

**Nothing is sacred!** Keep refining and tuning until you find something that is effective; and then continue to update it to keep it fresh and relevant to the changing marketplace and evolving client needs.

Look for ways to **form strategic alliances** or co-op with those companies or non-competitive sales reps who are already dealing with the people you would like to attract. Perhaps mine your on-line contacts for this?

What about those companies or reps who have already earned their trust and respect?

If you offer complimentary, non-competitive services or products that assist them in better serving their clients, you will find a more favorable response. You can return the favor with your clients.

Look for opportunities to offer this kind of connection to people who want to deal with your clients and who offer something you don't offer or are unable to do so profitably at this moment.

Who would you like to have as an alliance?
Who would you like to be referring business and sales to you?
Who can become your champion or fan?

*"To succeed in sales, simply talk to lots of people every day. And here's what's exciting - there are lots of people!"* **Jim Rohn**

# A foundation check-up – Are you getting ALL the sales you need?

Taking time to reflect on your performance and follow through is certainly time well invested.

- So how are things going?
- Are your sales figures where you expect them to be?
- Are you doing well in your conversion and closing ratios?

If your clients get the impression that you or your staff are indifferent to them or their needs, they will leave. Indifference can creep into even the best sales career or business. That perceived indifference 'will' cost you business.

**Are you getting all the sales or business you can?** If not, then a little honest self-inspection might be helpful. A few years back, a fellow sales professional shared some questions with me that I found extremely helpful. Thought I would pass them along for your reference and reflection.

**Take a minute and answer the following questions with a simple yes or no.**

**Mark yes with a (+) and no with a (-).**

Do you personally thank your internal customers – your team members and suppliers – for being a productive part of your business success?

Do you make sure they are well informed about new things happening in your business or affecting your industry?

Do you ever surprise them or reward them with a small gift or acknowledgement?

Do you make a point to stay in touch with current clients on a regular basis?

Do you normally follow up with clients shortly after they've dealt with you to ensure they are happy with their purchase or service?

Do you answer the phone on the second ring consistently?

Does a caller get asked for permission, if you need to put them on hold?

Do you ensure no one waits on hold for more than 30 seconds without checking to see if they can continue holding or dealing with their call?

Do you have an on-hold message for them to listen to?

Do you thank your clients or potential clients for calling you?

Do you thank them for buying from you?

If you are unsuccessful in helping them, do you thank them for the opportunity?

Do you and your staff arrive on time for any client appointments or meetings?

Do you or your team ever make your clients wait?

Do you consistently deliver products or services when agreed?

Do you let your clients know ASAP (before hand), if there is a problem?

Do you offer solutions or alternatives if there are any?

Do you return client calls and messages the same day they are received?

Does each team member make a commitment to take responsibility for helping clients or do they hand off client problems from department to department?

Do you ask for more information when you're asked about the price of a product or service?

Do you make sure you understand what they need your product or service for and that what they select is the best item or service to do the job?

Do you thank your clients or potential clients for coming in to visit your business?

Do you ask satisfied clients who they know who might also be able to use you?

Do you follow up on those referrals in a timely manner?

Do you and your staff meet on a regular basis to brainstorm better ways to serve your clients and for better ways of operating your business?

**There is no right or wrong in this check up**. However, the results to your questions can give you an indication of areas where you are potentially losing sales or missing opportunities to sell and service your clients more productively and profitably. Good luck and good selling.

### Idea-rich service as a sales tool for higher prices

If you are looking for a way to differentiate yourself from your completion and minimize having to offer discounts, exceptional customer service works. More so if you happen to be a smaller company (or project that smaller, friendly image to your prospective clients). As reported in a 2011 **American Express** survey 80% of North Americans thought that smaller companies placed a greater emphasis on customer service. In that survey respondents indicated (70%) they were willing to spend more with companies they believed provide excellent customer service. They also mentioned (59%) they'd try a new brand or company if it provided a better customer service experience.

**Think about who you do business with now.** For example, I drive out of my way to use a dry cleaner that treats me special. There are several other vendors that get my business because of their service. I don't mind the difference in price, because I know what I am getting, and I like it, and I like them.

As reported in a Customer Experience Impact report by **Harris Interactive**, 90% indicated they would pay 'more' to ensure they got a superior customer service.

Even if you are a BIG-BOX type of operation, simply competing on price is not the most effective way to build or sustain your business. Exceptional service delivered each time is a great defense against even the toughest competition – customer service that provides what they really need, delivered with expertise, and a great attitude. Make them feel special, treat them right, and they will come back to you and bring their friends.

# How much are you 'really' working?

If I asked how many of you were busy, I'd get close to 90% saying yes. If I asked how many were 'working' more than 50 hours a week, the answer might be 70% or more.

The critical question is, **"How many of you feel like you've effectively used your time during the last week?"** The answers here would be lower; less than 50% of respondents in my sessions thought they were using their time effectively. This lower response is one of the reasons for sharing these ideas.

The second reason was the knowledge that the best way to 'learn' something was to 'teach' it. And I really wanted to 'learn'! With my overloaded schedule and commitments, I was motivated to 'learn'. I wanted then, and still do, my freedom and control of my life and time.

One of the 'freedom' tools developed, in addition to my daily schedule, was the use of a simple log-book. I'd suggest creating one for your personal use. A friend who works as an accountant, told me she keeps something like this close at hand to track her 'billable' hours and found it helpful. I found it helped me track my 'productive' hours invested in my business.

It is invaluable as a periodic check-up on how I 'actually' allocate my time. A check on how much 'real work' was accomplished each day. A check up on how much time was spent with the important people in my life. A check up on how available hours are allocated to accomplishing life goals I've set.

Management expert, **Peter Drucker** was a strong advocate of this idea. Before planning on how one wishes to spend their time, he recommended you first need to know 'where' you are spending it. Made sense to me! This can be a sobering form, if you approach it openly and honestly. It will help you get a real grip on 'your' time wasters and help improve your overall effectiveness in managing your life and your time. It can be an indicator of misplaced values and a misguided sense of purpose.

**Luci Swindoll** wrote, *"Purpose or mission is determined by the development of values, balance, ethics, humor, morality, and sensitivities. It manifests itself in the way we look at life."*

**The best method I've found** is to simply go about your regular day making notes on the various activities you engage in during that day. For example:

- meetings
- conversations
- phone calls to clients
- pricing
- travel
- coffee and snack breaks
- drop in visitors
- sleeping
- childcare
- cooking
- daydreaming
- correspondence
- internet searches, and playing games on-line
- dealing with client problems
- personal errands
- TV
- entertainment
- talking with your spouse, or special someone
- spiritual time
- socializing
- phone calls
- client interviews
- job site
- commuting
- washroom activities
- eating
- housework
- shopping
- water cooler conferences
- research
- reading the paper
- reading work-related materials
- community work
- family time
- sports
- love making
- time with your kids
- other activities

**I think you get the idea.** On any given day, we are involved in a host of activities, the above list covering only some of them from experience. Many of you will have additions to this list.

Deliberately take a minute 'every half hour' and jot down what you did during that time. Don't stop to analyze it or try to artificially make it look good by justifying any action. At this point, simply record your use of time in 5, 10, or 15-minute increments. From experience, the half-hour record works better than every 15 minutes. Consider doing this for 3 to 5 days until you get the hang of it. Don't worry if you miss a few points. You are the only one who sees this check-in sheet.

At the end of your 'test' period, take your sheets and be brutally honest when looking at them. Total the activities by category.

For example, REAL WORK, family time, personal, filler time, wasted time, etc. I'm sure you'll see a trend appearing in how you really use your time and where you may be a bit less effective than you want to be.

**If you are aware of how you 'presently' use time, you will be better equipped to make the changes to make better use of it in the future.**

You'll have the opportunity to reflect and refine how you value your time and the activities in which you invest it. Do this periodically as a check up on how well you are now using your time, and to give you a sense of the areas where you still 'need' a little work!

Someone close to me told me, *"Show me how you spend your time and I'll know your values in life!"* What will your daily schedule - time log reveal about your choices in life? And once you've seen it, what will you do with the information?

You can break down or group the activities as needed for your own research. It doesn't have to be pretty, just accessible and easy to use. This is for your awareness only. Good Luck!

Visit: **www.SuccessPublications.ca**

*"People spend and excessive amount of time conjugating three verbs: 'To Want', 'To Have', and 'To Do'. We had forgotten that 'To Be' is the source and fount of life."* **Unknown**

## Service Still Sells

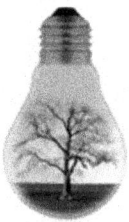

**Alfredo** is 'my' plumber; my go to guy for at least 12 years when I need something fixed or installed (2 bathrooms, a new kitchen, hot water heater, etc.); who is prompt, friendly, and really knows his trade. He is a friendly guy and I wouldn't think of hiring someone else. His wife, **Ursula,** had the *Crimson Creek Café* in nearby Redwater, Alberta (and my coffee spot). She made everyone feel welcome and took time to 'sell' the new additions to their coffee and sandwich collections. This was my place to drop in for a break in my routine, until health issues caused her to close. **Both know – service sells!**

# How much is your time 'really' worth?

Have you ever taken a moment and thought about what your time is *worth?* Have you ever calculated your earning capacity on an hourly basis? It can be a great exercise in determining your worth, relative value, and earning contribution. It can also tell you how much each minute or hour you allow to be wasted is really costing you.

**Let's figure out a typical time/value calculation.** A typical year with 2 vacation weeks and 10 holidays leaves us with only 240 workdays in which to earn our living. Assuming an average 8-hour workday this gives us **1920 potential work hours in a year.** On the surface, we'd simply take our Gross Pay and divide by the hours, e.g. $50,000/year would give us an average hourly rate of $26.04 per hour. So, in this instance each 15-minute block of **wasted time would be costing you $6.51. Work it out for your salary or earnings level to see the value of YOUR time!**

Let's take this a bit further, shall we? **In all honesty, would you say that you are able to get 8 productive hours in each 8-hour day?** Of course not! Honest feedback from quite a few of our North American audience members puts the 'true number' somewhere closer **to a generous 60% effectiveness on any given day.** I know some of you are saying, *"I only wish I had a 60% rate."* If that is true, then we really have only 1152 work hours in which to make our money. In the example above, each hour would now be worth $43.04 and each 15-minute block costing us $10.85.

Most of us would not deliberately waste a full day, but often let 15-minute segments slip away without notice or regret. This is one of the foundation points of success as a leader. **Take back your time and choose to invest it in your growth and in that of your team.**

Here are some rough comparisons in our table for different dollar earning levels.

| Annual Rate | Base Rate | Effective Rate (60%) | 15-minute block |
|---|---|---|---|
| 50,000/year | $26.04 | $43.40 | $10.85 |
| 100,000/year | $52.08 | $86.80 | $21.70 |
| 200,000/year | $104.16 | $173.60 | $43.40 |

**Very interesting figures, aren't they?** If you remain aware of what your time is 'really' worth it will help you keep an eye on the time wasters that creep into your life. Not that I put a monetary price on everything in my life; but it is good to know what my *investment* or *contribution* is worth. I invoice my no-fee or reduced clients showing the real value (showing the discount or gift) of what I just *gave* them. This is as much for me as them.

*After my dad died, I spent quite a lot of time with my mom before she passed away. It was probably the best return for my investment I've ever made – priceless!* **I'd do it again in a heartbeat if I could.**

Our objective here is not to focus on the money, but to allow it to remind you how 'valuable' your time really is as a leader.

When working with executives and their teams on liberating time, we challenge them to focus on liberating (saving) **5 to 15-minute blocks** of time from their over-committed schedules. Their objective is creating at least one or more 15-minute block a day. Those 15-minute choices (segments) can be very valuable when focused on your more important priorities, one of which would be *working* with your teams.

Based on an improved age span of 85 years, we have **ONLY 31,046 days to LIVE!** Roughly 745,000 hours in which to live out our dreams, accomplish our life goals, create our legacy of leadership, and make an impact on our world and those with whom we share it. My bet many of you reading this are at least a quarter of the way down your path. Time is moving quickly, and we have critical choices to make. According to Goethe, ***"One always has enough time, provided one spends it well."*** What difference would that make?

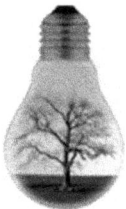

### What makes 'YOU-nique?'

***"To my customer, I may not have the answer, but I'll find it.
I may not have the time, but I'll make it.
I may not be the biggest, but I'll be the most committed
to your success!"*** **Anonymous**

In a world of increasing 'me-too's' and 'sorta-like's' and 'ditto's' - what makes you stand out from the crowd? What **'YOU-niqueness'** do you bring to the marketplace that will make your potential customers want to deal with you and return time and time again?

# Mistakes made by new or ineffective sales staff

Why is it 'some' senior sales staff are more effective, profitable, and productive in their selling efforts?

Why are some sales staff better at building long-term profitable relationships with clients that result in repeat sales? Could it be that they've learned these simple points that help them sell better?

As we have learned in our studies, companies that take care of their clients generally keep them over a longer period. **Companies who train and equip their selling staff generally keep them longer as well.** But there are some pitfalls here as well, for ineffective sales staff, or newer sales personals who lack the proper training.

*"The difference between greatness and mediocrity is often how an individual views a mistake."* **Nelson Boswell**

## Here are areas where they often fall short

**Lack of preparation.** There is an old saying: "Success happens when opportunity meets preparedness!" This impacts your credibility and the establishment of a trust relationship with a client.

**Not listening.** 90% of salespeople don't listen effectively and are doomed to ineffectiveness. Active listening is the key foundation to discovering what your client needs, and will need, and being able to serve them.

**Failing to ask for the order.** Most of the studies show that 70% of all sales folks NEVER ask for the order. An even larger percentage never ask for additional orders. Do yours?

**Poor or no follow up.** Follow up and follow through is where 90% of all great sales are made. Conversely, this is where most sales staff lose the opportunity to gain and maintain a client.

**Small thinking.** Want bigger sales? You must think and act bigger. Ask these questions: "How high is high? What is my maximum potential?" "What is the lifetime value of my relationship with this client?" "What is the potential for referrals from this client?"

**Failing to establish and/or maintain rapport.** This can be a killer if you are committed to maintaining a mutually profitable relationship over a long period of time with your clients.

**Failing to really commit and establish themselves as experts in their field.** People like to deal with and talk about people who 'know' what they are doing. This impacts your future earnings with clients.

## Ask yourself how you fare on each of these areas

- Would you give yourself a passing mark?
- Which ones would need a little work?
- How will you change to make sure you give your customers the most professional service possible?
- Focus on improvement in each of these areas and see your sales soar.

**A note to Managers:** Give your team a chance to win by reminding them of these success tactics. Remind them to keep focused and keep working toward their goals of helping the client make a decision that is good for their client and profitable over the long haul for the company. How can you help them make the changes they need to become a professional salesperson and provide continued value-added service?

**"Many salespeople are 'ASK' resistant – they are afraid to ask for the sale. And, as a result, they fail to meet or exceed their full potential in the sales arena."**

*I remember spending the day with 200 plus salespeople in Wisconsin. I worked with half of them in the morning, their sales managers at lunch, and the remainder following lunch. This was part of helping this leading state-wide furniture retailer launch their version of our on-line **Secret Selling Tip sales success program.***

*As a part of my presentation, I asked them if anyone wanted to know a secret that would 'guarantee' they would generate two to three times more sales in the coming year. Hands went up all over the room. I asked them to get their pens ready to write down this amazing secret and I could see them anxiously awaiting my next words. I paused dramatically and said, **"Simply ask for the order (sale) at least twice in every sales conversation."** I watched with amazement as faces showed their disappointment. They had been expecting some life changing answer. I had given it to them, but many of them did not hear it. I went on to say, "Many of you do not even ask for the order once and your results show it. One of their more productive sales ladies told me I had nailed it."*

# Proactive strategies to minimize price objections

## How do you compete when you know you aren't the least expensive in your area or industry?

How do you compete in an increasingly competitive global market?

**Here are a few areas that will help in this regard.**

### Conduct a Strategic Value Analysis

Taking the time to find out a bit about these four areas will help you build a strong foundation and relationship to better service your customers. Better relationships will take the pressure of the price factor in the buying decision. The more you know, the better you can apply that knowledge in serving those who need what you provide.

**Market Analysis**
**Competitive Analysis**
**Self-analysis**
**Customer analysis**

### Positioning Strategies - to create barriers

The more successful companies have carved out a position as the quality leader in their field.

This emphasis on quality or value moves the evaluation process away from price and enhances your chances of a sale.

### Outsmart the competition

Use your brains and look for ways to better service your customers. Find ways to provide services or value-added products that your competition doesn't.

### Use/leverage all your resources

Being lean and mean in using/leveraging your resources helps you to keep your overhead in line and keep your pricing competitive. Using your resources fully allows you to better serve them as well.

## Decide on all organizational needs

Invest the time to streamline your operation and its processes. Keep it simple! This will help your staff provide the best service possible. It also allows your customers to see firsthand your commitment to giving them value for their dollar. Think repeat, long-term business! Check out **"Think Beyond the FIRST Sale"** from www.SuccessPublications.ca

## Work to generate end-user support

If you are in the position of being a supplier – your customers are really your 'customers' customers (end users). How can you help your customers by working to reach and teach the end users? Become a drawing point or success partner for your customers.

## Value-added Checklist (10 minimum - go for 20)

*"The individual (the customer) perceives service in his or her own terms."* **Arch McGill**

### Bundling

How about making what you offer more valuable by combining products or services to allow your customers lots of options. What types of bundles can you offer? Take a moment and brainstorm ideas.

### Proactive probing

Invest the time to find out what moves your customers? What keeps them up at night? Ask questions and respond to what you learn, by adapting or changing your business. This keeps what you offer current, valuable, and viable.

### Reinforce value

Everything you do should be focused on reinforcing the value in what you offer. What is the true value of what you offer? Warranty, service, selection, delivery, options?

### Sell intangibles

Often the true value of what you sell is based on things that can't be shown or proven until needed, as above.

Do you have a better warranty? Do you offer better terms? Do you offer a better selection or stocking? Do you offer expert advice or consulting? Do you offer delivery and installation? Let them know! Don't be shy about sharing your unique value proposition. If you are shy – you'll die in a competitive market.

## Presentation ideas

When you get an opportunity to present or share about your business or products – I'd suggest looking for ways to incorporate the following areas into your sales process. You can be a great spokesman if you do. This will also be a tremendous assist in helping them decide to deal with you – closing can be a challenge. But these hints will help you be more effective in signing up additional business and retaining clients.

## How can you…?

Demonstrate earnings
Cut/reduce/minimize their costs
Go for agreement to product/service first
Carefully choose your words
Use proper descriptive sales terms instead of jargon
Sandwich the price - focus on value (good, better, best!)
Price with benefits summary
Cost as a 'mere' fraction
Minimize the cost-to-own
Analogize – not apologize
Use relevant testimonials where ever possible
Think and talk 'long-term'
Present deal in its best light

These critical impact areas are essential to be a value-based customer service business. Look for ways to build them into your business. The effort you invest will pay off – BIG TIME, and long-term!

*"If people offer their help and wisdom as you go through life, accept it gratefully. You can learn much from those who have gone before you."* **Edmund O'Neill**

# Motivation and encouragement

Live your DREAMS whatever they may be...

*"Surround yourself with those who believe in you and will help you achieve your goals."* **Lisa Marie Yost**

When you are struggling, and that happens to each of us, remember to apply the wisdom in this quote. As someone once said, ***"the best time to dig a well is before you are thirsty."***

Building a valued support network is a worthy activity if your desire is long term success and growth. These valued friends, coaches, cheerleaders, and champions will help you weather the storms and detours life puts in your way. Invest time along the way building your network and remember it works both ways. You have the responsibility of being there for them as well.

**Life can be challenging at times.** Careers and businesses go through dips and detours. Make sure to keep focused on your goals and dreams. Having a supportive network will help in this regard. I am so blessed with the amazing people in my life. My wife, my friends, my colleagues, and my clients who invite me into their organizations to share my ideas.

# Affirmations & visualization
*The POWER of positive self-talk*

Medal winning Olympic athletes, award winning actors, writers, creative people, and, yes, even successful public and professional speakers have learned the power of self-talk through affirmations and the applied use of visualization techniques. These tools help them to see themselves performing at their best or presenting in a positive manner and enjoy the sense of accomplishment in advance.

**Visualization is simple.** Take a moment and imagine yourself walking confidently to the front of the room, enjoying thunderous applause as you are introduced. Imagine walking up the stairs to the stage and shaking hands with your MC. Then imagine turning, taking a moment to make eye contact with the audience, as you ground yourself and take a few deep breaths. You smile, and the audience smiles back at you! You feel accepted and confident! You visibly see and feel their support and encouragement. You begin your presentation with a strong clear voice and sense the excitement flowing through the crowd as your opening captivates their attention.

As you continue to speak, you experience them laughing with you. Your heart soars with excitement. You skilfully lead them through the points you've outlined, and you can see them 'getting your message!' You lead up to a powerful conclusion and end with a call to action that brings them to their feet clapping and cheering. You bask in the warmth of their appreciation and smile at them. As you return to your seat, you realize you never even had to look at your notes. You did great!

**Visualization allows your mind to experience the event** before you perform it. The amazing thing is it can be so vivid, that when you get up to present you are more relaxed, because you've already done it.

*It works very well, as I found out when I was preparing for each of my three performances in the accredited speaker program. I did this prior to leaving for the Toastmasters International conferences in San Diego, St. Louis, and finally Palm Desert. I also checked out the room where I would be presenting and did a quick run through of my presentation in the room. Finally, when I had a chance, I practiced walking across the main stage to receive my plaque as a professional level Accredited Speaker (way back in 1995). In August 1998, on an extremely hot sunny day, I walked across that stage in Palm Desert, CA to receive my professional level Accredited Speaker designation following the World Championships.*

*I wondrously experienced, for real, the emotions I had earlier imagined, to the thunderous roar of applause, whistles, and cheers of over 2000 Toastmasters from around the world.* **I had been there before – in my imagination FOUR years earlier.**

Visualization is the secret to seeing and achieving your goals as a successful leader or speaker. How do you keep yourself positive as you journey toward your goal? **Positive self-talk and affirmations** will work wonders to keep you focused and on track to your success.

Affirmations work by **'speaking the truth, as you would see it'** to your mind and your heart. To be effective, affirmations must possess these three criteria:

- They must be **positive!**
- They must be in the **present tense** (today).
- And they must be **personal**.

Here are some ideas I've used over the years. Create your own, make them yours, and use them, as needed, daily for best results. I've used them individually or as groups. Create what works for you.

Having some instrumental music playing in the background helps me relax and enhances the experience. Try this for yourself when things are quiet and when you won't be disturbed. Let these ideas germinate in your mind.

- My breathing is relaxed and effortless
- My heartbeat is slow and regular
- My muscles are relaxed and warm
- I feel at peace… I am at peace
- I am aware that I am a unique and special person
- Now is the best time to be alive… I am glad I am alive!
- I give the best of myself in everything I undertake!
- I keep the commitments I make
- I earn the respect of others
- I have a sense of adventure
- I have a sense of excitement!
- I am enjoying my work and the success I've earned
- I see new opportunities each day
- I am gentle… I demonstrate my caring for others

- I take time to play like a child… I enjoy my life
- I am strong… I am a winner!!!
- Today is the best day of my life… so far
- I thank GOD for His many gifts to me
- I encourage and support others in achieving their goals
- I am confident in my abilities and skills!
- I inspire confidence from my audiences!
- I grow friendships… I am a true friend
- I look for new ways to give value to my audiences
- I grow relationships with people I'd like to spend time with and learn from
- I offer a service that improves the quality of other's lives, to increase their wealth, well-being, and happiness
- I remember my presentation without pause or need of notes
- I know my subject and have selected that which is most valuable to share
- I am prepared, practiced, and polished for my presentation today!!!
- I will give each presentation as though it were my last
- I am excited about the opportunity to share my Ideas At Work!
- I will live my life today as though it was my last
- I will laugh and share my love with each person I meet

Try these on for size; change them or add to this list as you discover what is truly important for you. **Positive self-talk works. Listen to your heart!**

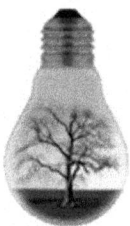

### Master the power of training

Regaining your freedom means passing along some of those 'non-vital' things to others by effective delegation. Right now, I bet you can think of at least three activities you hate that you haven't 'had time' to train someone else to do. Right?

**Make the time!** Until you do, you will never be free. Invest a day now to train and hand off at least one of these items. This will save you un-countless hours as you move forward and allow you to focus on your 'vital few' activities that move you forward.

# Each Life a Legacy – Live on Purpose!

*Our life and leadership are a portrait of who we are – autograph yours with style!*

*Whether we realize it or not, our life and leadership leave a legacy. People we know, lead, work, or live with will have a lasting impression based on their experience with us.*

*Why is it we wait until they are gone to acknowledge the important people in our life? Life is a choice, as is leadership.*

I've lived in the country north-east of Edmonton, Alberta for the past 18 years. It is a quieter, more rustic type of life. As I drive the rural highways, I see scenes like this one. What used to be homes, inhabited by families with dreams. Homes left to fall apart, torn and worn by the winds and the rain. Homes left to the elements when the people who used to live there moved on. Houses, that have become interesting pictures of broken-down buildings in a field. I wonder what happened. Yet, I see some older homes, lovingly cared for, passed on from father/mother to son/daughter, family-to-family, still vibrant with life. As I drive though smaller towns, I see vacant buildings that used to house thriving businesses. What makes the difference, I wonder?

**What legacy will you leave behind?** When your time is done in your current role, or here on earth, what legacy would you like to leave? What picture would you like your team, your co-leaders, and the community to remember about your work and/or your life? What would be the ultimate comment on your life and contributions?

## Why not leave a legacy that has contributed in a positive way?

Once we understand that we leave a legacy behind, we can make a conscious choice to make sure it is a positive one. We can choose to invest our time, resources, and energies in those activities and those organizations that create lasting value and in the lives of those we love and respect.

113

As leaders, we have that opportunity to invest in the lives of those we lead. That investment can leave a legacy in their productive lives and the lives of those they touch.

*My parents both left us in 1999. Their death left a big hole in the lives of my sister and me. But, more importantly, they left a legacy of love and commitment to community involvement that has been ingrained in our lives. Their legacy lives on in our lives and our contributions.*

## Acknowledging the accomplishments and contributions of those around us!

Over the years I've learned that people too often die unacknowledged and unappreciated. This is one of the biggest losses in our rich culture and legacy as a nation. We have people who have made an impact in our lives, who have made a difference too, and they don't know – because we never told them!

**Resolve to tell people now** and tell them often how important they are in your lives and where they have made a difference. It can be the most valuable gift you can give. This can be such a wonderful legacy as a leader – to tell people now how you appreciate them and their contributions; to share positive encouragement as they seek to grow in their respective roles. Pick up a phone, drop an email, write a note! **Now!** Come back to this book later.

## Investing in the lives of others can be our best legacy!

I've often heard, *"You can't take it with you!"* Interesting thought! In one sense, it is true. When we pass away, we leave everything we once held important behind. *"I've yet to see a hearse pulling a U-Haul trailer."* When we take personal leadership with our time and resources, we can re-invest them in the people we want to help now and in those who might be joining us one day.

Think of all the people who have invested in your life and your success to date. Some have passed away, but their investment in you is still paying dividends as you continue to grow and pass on what they taught you. You have that opportunity to 'pay it forward' for your team members, family, and communities. The most important activity and use of time is investing in our team for their success on the job. As leaders, this is our best gift!

## Realize the impact you have and choose to make it a dynamic one!

We make an impact on the lives of others each day and in each encounter, we have with them. We have an impact on strangers and on people who we may not even know. Like the ripples on a lake that bounce off each other, we do have an impact; and we change the patterns of those we connect with, as do those who connect with us.

One of the most decisive and productive decisions I made was to undertake to make a difference in my life, to leave a positive legacy behind me. To leave a legacy of empowered and encouraged people, audiences, readers, and family and friends who knew I loved and cared enough to give my very best. Who know I believed in them and prayed for their success in life. To make sure my words, written and verbal were based in truth, delivered in love, and focused on the positive opportunities in life. Thank you for investing your time with me in this personal leadership development book. I truly value each of you and the time we spend together over the miles.

*"Lord willing, I have a few more productive years ahead. ☺ I still have book ideas to birth, countries I want to visit with Irene; and friends around the world I have not met yet. But, regardless of the time He allows me, I pray that when I go, I leave a legacy as rich as those of my parents Ron and Marge Hooey. I would be blessed indeed if I was able to leave that kind of legacy behind."*

## What will you leave behind as a legacy of how you invested your time?

*"There are always two choices, two paths to take. One is easy and that is its only reward."*
**Unknown**

# The Power of ONE!

## Ever thought... I'm only one person, what can I do?

*I met Ashley and Porsha Demyen in 2005 when they were 9 and 11 respectively. These two young ladies dramatically answered that question recently when they announced they'd met and surpassed their goal of raising $10,000 for Edmonton's Support Network.*

Their goal began that fall when they shared the thought of doing something to put their handprint on the community and caught the vision for helping people who hurt in Edmonton. Their mom worked at The Support Network and acted as their assistant, along with their dad. They hand wrote appeal letters and sent them out... the response was amazing... and on April 18th, 2005 (Ashley's 9th birthday) they presented a check to **The Support Network** for $10,000.

*As I sat in that audience (quietly wiping the 'wetness' that was leaking from my eyes) I thought, "If an 9 and 11-year-old can do that... what can I do, what can we as adults do, if we decide to commit and follow through on that commitment?"*

Edmonton's **Bill Comrie** praised their achievement at a Support Network fundraising event – **Theresia Comrie Champagne Lunch**, at which he was the special guest speaker.

*I frequently have people ask me, 'As a motivational speaker... how do you keep motivated?' Well, this is one of the ways... being open to the stories of those around me who reach out and move mountains in their lives. Allowing myself to be touched by their stories, moved by their actions and inspired by their personal legends and legacies. We are surrounded by un-assuming heroes and inspirational people who simply see a need and decide to do something about it... and act on that decision. Thanks Ashley and Porsha... you continue to inspire me!*

### My challenge for you is twofold:

1) Look around and see who might be acting in this role in your life and tell them you appreciate their leadership and inspiration.

2) See what you can do in your own life and role to reach out and make a difference.

**What makes a champion?**

- Is it winning against all odds?
- Is it continuing when others have told you to quit?
- Is it doing your best and giving it your all?
- Is it pushing past your comfort zone into the darkness to learn your limits?

Ask 20-year-old, legally blind, Iditarod musher **Rachael Scdoris** from Bend, Oregon who competed in the 2005 race. For those who may not know, this is a 1,100-mile journey through darkness from Anchorage to Nome, Alaska. Only the hardy or the fool hearty attempt it. Only the toughest competitors make any headway, some finish, and only one wins. Rachael and her sled team made 700 gruelling miles on this trek before concern for her dogs forced her to withdraw. *(They had contracted viral infection and weren't eating.)* Rachael was already planning her 2006 race. **That is determination and that is being a champion.**

*Note: 2006 she became the 1ˢᵗ legally blind person to complete the 1049+ mile Iditarod Trail Sled Dog Race.*

When asked why she did this, she was characteristically open. In Rachael's own words, *"I refused to sit back and let life quietly slip past me."* She continued in her autobiography, *"I want to live and experience everything I possibly can. I know there are dangers out there. I accept them. No, I embrace them. Dangers present us with fear... and fear is my fuel. If I did not meet the dangers of this world head on and come to grips with my fear, I would be cheating myself."*

**That is the heart of a champion!**

- What dangers and fears do you face in your life, your career or in building your business?
- What plans have you made to confront them and to tackle them head on?

# How to Handle the Idea Killers in Your Life!

**YOU** have this great dream or this fantastic idea bursts into your head. You're excited about the unlimited possibilities and can't wait to share it with your co-workers, closest friends, and, of course, your family.

**What is their reaction?** All too often, their initial reaction is to ridicule the idea, to point out its flaws, to remind you about your lack of education, your lack of money, your lack of experience, or to point out how so and so tried it and it didn't work. Whew! The result ... too often, you stop and let your dreams die, be minimized, or give up on your ideas. You've let your colleagues, friends, and family opinions and criticism 'rob' you of your future and your solid potential for greatness!

**Why do they do that?** Well, it might be for a variety of reasons, some of them with the best intentions. It might simply be their concern to see you avoid getting hurt or to side step what they see as a path to failure.

It may be, and often is, based on their 'own fears' projected onto your action and life. It might be due to a personal failure on their part and a fear that, if you succeed, they will lose you. Or a fear they will have to deal with the reality that, just maybe, they could have done something about their 'seemingly impossible' situation. Your potential for success scares them or makes them a bit nervous about their own chances, neglect, or inactivity.

How do we handle these 'helpers' or **'idea killers'** in our life? One of the best ways is to be aware of their existence and seek to avoid them in areas of vulnerability. I don't mean to cut them off completely. Just realize that they are not committed to or understanding of your dreams and desires. Be kind, as they do not know that they don't get it. Don't waste your energy on them. Make a conscious choice to keep these areas private, especially during the embryonic or incubation stages of establishing your goals, dreams, or ideas. Maintain your focus and keep moving forward to see your idea or dream become a reality.

As someone once wrote, **"Show no regrets for the past, no fear for the future. Expect to win – expect GREATNESS!"**

**It's a funny thing in life, if you refuse to accept anything but the best, you often get it!** We may not get to choose our family, but we do have full control over our friends and over the amount of time we spend with colleagues, friends, and family. This is where we make the decisions and connections that help shape or determine our destiny.

In life, there are those who would kill our dreams and those who would, if asked, help nurture our dreams. We can identify and choose each group in which to associate and productively invest our time. Find your champions!

One of the most effective ways of dealing with an idea killer is by **doing your homework**. If you have researched your dream and have done your due diligence, some can even be brought around to being 'at least' a neutral observer. And, when you succeed, watch them come out then!

Use feedback from these idea killers as *mirrors* that may show you your 'blind spots'. Often, they see things that you might miss in the heat of passion. Keep in mind their input is for **information 'only'** and check it for relevance and accuracy before you allow it to impact or influence your decisions.

**Demonstrate by your strategic actions** that you're committed to seeing 'this' project through to completion. Often our past track record of starting and not completing projects may influence their support and enthusiasm. This is especially true with immediate family members.

**Idea killers may occasionally become allies**, but it takes massive work on your part to win them over to your team. Keep focused on your Goals and Dreams! Don't let another person's critical attitude determine your worth or your future. Don't let them stop you! You don't know how high you can fly until you spread your wings and take to the sky. Please don't let another person's limiting beliefs, no matter how well-intentioned, stop you attempting to dream big, to compete for the ultimate prize, achieving your personal or professional dream. Create the future you imagine!

It is too easy for those around you, who are hopelessly mired in their own mediocrity, to criticize you for trying to follow your dream or acting to implement your great idea.

# I dare you!

Remember growing up and being dared to do something? Remember how often you accomplished it, despite your own self doubts and fears? Well, I want to share a big DARE. But first, let me tell you the quick story of a young man named Bill who responded to a personal DARE and changed his world and perhaps ours as well.

Bill was not a healthy boy; in fact, you might even have called him 'sickly'. His family moved from the country to the city where he encountered a teacher who was serious about health. As he wrote later, *'It was like he had singled me out.'* His teacher, George Krall challenged him one day. He looked straight at Bill and said, *"I dare you to be the healthiest boy in class!"*

Young Bill responded and soon built a body that equalled and outlasted the strongest boys in his class. In fact, he never lost a day at work because of illness and lived a healthy and productive life. He served honourably during the 1st World War and returned to lead his fledgling company to greater success and profit during the great depression. He passed away in 1955, at 85, when the average life expectancy was a good 20 years lower, in part because he responded to that dare.

Bill launched a company which grew to be one of North America's largest corporations, providing employment for thousands of people. People who were challenged or dared by their president and later Chairman of the Board to push themselves to be strong, to be creative, to take risks, to build character, and to share with others. For nearly 40 years, Bill wrote a weekly inspirational *"Monday Morning Message"* for his employees, colleagues and associates.

In a 1955 Monday Morning Message, when he was 84, he pointed out the personal significance of some of these unchanging fundamentals. *"Some folks are continually making changes,"* he said. *"I flatter myself that I like new ventures and new experiences. But when it comes to fundamentals, I believe in finding the right foundations and building on them. I'm a poor changer. For instance, here are some of the fundamentals I have never changed: I have been a church member for over 60 years; married to one wife for over 60 years; a lodge member for over 60 years; and a Purina man for over 60 years."*

Young Bill in this story is, of course, **William H. Danforth**, founder of the Ralston Purina Company, founder of the American Youth Foundation Camps, and author of 14 books including, **"I Dare You!"**

The copy I bought in 1976 was in its 26th printing. Bill Danforth's life and his writings have challenged hundreds of thousands (*including me*) to live life as an adventure and to stretch and grow in our careers and in our service to others.

I want to leave you with the following personal challenge:

## I Dare You:

- To **believe** in yourself, your experience, and your skills
- To **push** yourself to learn and hone your skills for greater success
- To **invest** in at least one course every quarter to enhance your skills
- To **take** increased responsibility and personal leadership in your role
- To **tap** into your creativity and allow innovation to flow
- To **support** and encourage your fellow team members to grow
- To **never** allow anyone or anything to stop you from succeeding in your role and in life.

And **I dare you to be the example for others in living life as an adventure and pushing past your comfort zone into the winner's zone.**

**PRO-TIP:** Helping someone believe in themselves can be the first, vitally important step, in motivating a person. If someone is unable to even 'see' what they are capable of accomplishing or believing in themselves to successfully reach a goal or make a positive change, our ability to motivate is useless. Perhaps the most power four words we can speak to someone is, "I believe in you". We must help that person more clearly understand that they already possess everything they need to successfully accomplish a goal, if only they will believe that it is possible. For many, if we speak these words to them, with sincerity and conviction, it may be the only time they have ever heard these life-changing words. To successfully motivate another, we must reach into the core of who they are and build that foundation of belief from within. Once we build that element of self-confidence, their ability of motivating themselves will know no bounds.

© *Tammy Miller,* PID, AS, DTM www.TammySpeaks.com

# Copyright and license notes

'**Prepare Yourself to WIN!** (Updated 3rd edition)
*Idea-rich success secrets*

**Bob 'Idea Man' Hooey**, Accredited Speaker, 2011 Spirit of CAPS recipient.
Prolific author of 30 plus business, leadership, and career success publications

Cover design: **Wendy** (craftarc)
Photos of Bob: **Dov Friedman**, www.photographybyDov.com
Photos of Bob: **Frédéric Bélot,** www.fredericbelot.fr/fr
Editorial, layout and design: **Irene Gaudet**, Vitrak Creative Services
(a division of Creativity Corner Inc.), vitrakcreative.com

**ISBN: 978-1-896737-95-9**

Printed in the United States 10 9 8 7 6 5 4 3 2 1
**Success Publications** – a division of Creativity Corner Inc.
Box 10, Egremont, AB T0A 0Z0
www.successpublications.ca
Creative office: 1-780-736-0009 (MST)

# Acknowledgements, credits, and disclaimers

As with each of my books, a very special dedication of this piece of myself, to the two people who meant the most to me, my folks **Ron and Marge Hooey**. Sadly, both my parents left this earthly realm in 1999. I still miss our time together and your encouragement and love. I was blessed with the two of you in my life. I've added **George and Lillian Sidor** (Irene's folks) to this gratitude list.

תודה
Dankie Gracias
Спасибо Merci Takk شکراً
Köszönjük Terima kasih
Grazie Dziękujemy Děkojame
Ďakujeme Vielen Dank Paldies
Kiitos Täname teid 謝謝
**Thank You** Tak
感謝您 Obrigado Teşekkür Ederiz
Σας Ευχαριστούμ 감사합니다
Bedankt Děkujeme vám ขอบคุณ
ありがとうございます
Tack

To my inspiring wife and professional proof-reader and publications coach, **Irene Gaudet**, who loves, encourages, and supports me in my quest to continue sharing my **Ideas At Work!** across the world. Thank you seems so inadequate for your timely work in helping make my writing and my client service better! I love the time we spend together!

To my colleagues and friends in the National Speakers Association (NSA), the Canadian Association of Professional Speakers (CAPS), and the Global Speakers Federation (GSF) who continually challenge me to strive for success and increased excellence.

To my great audiences, leaders, students, coaching clients, and readers across the globe who share their experiences and enjoyment of my work. Your positive and supportive feedback encourages me to keep working on additional programs and success publications like this updated version. My experience with you creates the foundation for additional real-life experiences I can take from the stage to the page, the classroom to the boardroom.

My thanks to a select few friends for your ongoing support and 'constructive' abuse. You know who you are. ☺

Special thanks to all our experts for their **PRO-TIPS**: In order of appearance in the book

*Wayne Land, Lindsay Adams, Faith Wood, Patricia Katz, Greg Gazin, Darren Lacroix, Sheryl Roush, Linda Maul, Joe Calloway, Phillip Van Hooser, Randy Gage, Shirley Borrelli, Dilip R. Abayasekara, Steve Lowell, Charmaine Hammond & Rebecca Kirstein, Kim Duke, Tammy Miller*

# Disclaimer

*We have not attempted to cite all the authorities and sources consulted in the preparation of this book. To do so would require much more space than is available. The list would include departments of various governments, libraries, industrial institutions, periodicals, and many individuals. Inspiration was drawn from many sources, including other books by the author; in this updated creation of* **"Prepare Yourself to WIN!'**

*This book is written and designed to provide information on more effective use of your time, as a life and leadership enhancement guide. It is sold with the 'explicit' understanding that the publisher and/or the author are not engaged in rendering legal, accounting, or other Professional services. If legal or other expert assistance is required, the services of a competent Professional in your geographic area should be sought.*

*It is not the purpose of this book to reprint all the information that is otherwise available. Its primary purpose is to complement, amplify, and supplement other books and reference materials already available. You are encouraged to search out and study all the available material, learn as much as possible, and tailor the information to your individual needs. This will help to enhance your success in being a more effective salesperson, leader or professional.*

*Every effort has been made to make this book as complete and as accurate as possible within the scope of its focus. However, there may be mistakes, both typographical and in content or attribution. Graphics are royalty free or under license. Care has been taken to trace ownership of copyright material contained in this volume. The publisher will gladly receive information that will allow him to rectify any reference, copyright, or credit line in subsequent editions. This book should be used only as a general guide and not as the ultimate source of information. Furthermore, this book contains information that is current only up to the date of publication.*

*The purpose of 'Prepare Yourself To WIN! is to educate and entertain; perhaps to inform and to inspire. It is certainly to challenge its readers to learn and apply its secrets and tips, to challenge them to enhance their skills and leverage their time to create more Productive outcomes. The author and publisher shall have neither liability nor responsibility to any person or entity with respect to any loss or damage caused, or alleged to have been caused, directly or indirectly, by the information contained in this book.*

# Bob's B.E.S.T. 'idea-rich' publications

**Bob 'Idea Man' Hooey** is a prolific author who has been capturing and sharing his wisdom and experience in print and electronic formats for the past fifteen plus years. In addition to the following publications, several of them best sellers, he has written for consumer, corporate, professional associations, trade, and on-line publications. He has been engaged to write and assist on publications by other best-selling writers and successful companies.

His publications are listed to give you an idea of the scope and topics he writes about.

Bob's **B**usiness **E**nhancement **S**uccess **T**ools

## Leadership, business, and career success series
- **Running TOO Fast** (8th edition 2019)
- **Legacy of Leadership** (3rd edition 2022)
- **Make ME Feel Special!** (6th edition 2022)
- **Why Didn't I 'THINK' of That?** (5th edition 2022)
- **Speaking for Success!** (10th edition 2023)
- **THINK Beyond the First Sale** (3rd edition 2023)
- **Prepare Yourself to WIN!** (3rd edition 2023)

## Bob's mini-book success series
- **The Courage to Lead!** (4th edition 2017)
- **Creative Conflict** (3rd edition 2017)
- **Get to YES!** (3rd edition 2017)
- **THINK Before You Ink!** (3rd edition 2017)
- **Running to Win!** (2nd edition 2017)
- **How to Generate More Sales** (4th edition 2017)
- **Unleash your Business Potential** (3rd edition 2017)

- **Learn to Listen** (2nd edition 2017)
- **Creativity Counts!** (3rd edition 2016)
- **Create Your Future!** (3rd edition 2017)
- **Thanks Mom!**
- **Dad, You're Still My Hero!**

## Bob's Pocket Wisdom series
- Pocket Wisdom for Selling Professionals
- Pocket Wisdom for Speakers (updated for 2019)
- Pocket Wisdom for Innovators
- Pocket Wisdom for Leaders – Power of One! (updated for 2019)
- Pocket Wisdom for Business Builders
- Additional PW books are coming in 2018-2019

## Co-authored books created by Bob
- Quantum Success – 3 volume series (2006)
- In the Company of Leaders (3rd edition 2014)
- Foundational Success (2nd edition 2013)

**Visit: www.SuccessPublications.ca** for more information on Bob's publications and other success resources.

### PRO-TIP: Leaders, Managers, Owners

We'd suggest this book, and some of the others listed above, might be a great reference and discussion guide for you and your team. Work through it and discuss where it is relevant in your specific staff focus, client interaction and culture. Working to create a client centered culture will pay dividends for years to come.

We have **'Prepare Yourself to WIN!'** available for bulk purchase as well as a lower investment E-pub (Kindle) version as well. Why not get each team member their own copy of either the print or E-pub version? If you'd like to make a print bulk order, please contact me and we'll work something out, just for you.

**Email: bob@ideaman.net or visit: www.SuccessPublications.ca**

# What they say about Bob 'Idea Man' Hooey

As I travel across North America, and more recently around the globe, sharing my Ideas At Work!, I am fortunate to get feedback and comments from my audiences and colleagues. These comments come from people who have been touched, challenged, or simply enjoyed themselves in one of my sessions.

**I'd love to come and share some ideas with your organization and teams.**

*"I've known Bob for several years and follow his activities in business with interest. I originally met Bob when he spoke for a Rotary Leadership Institute and got to know him better when he came to Vladivostok, Russia to speak to our leadership. When you spoke, I thought you were one of us because you talked about our challenges just like yours. You could understand the others, which makes you a great speaker!"* **Andrey Konyushok**, Rotary International District 2225 Governor 2012-2013, far eastern Russia

*"I still get comments from people about your presentation. Only a few speakers have left an impression that lasts that long. You hit a spot with the tourism people."* **Janet Bell**, Yukon Economic Forums

*"We greatly appreciate the energy and effort you put into researching and adapting your keynote to make it more meaningful to our member councils. Early feedback from our delegates indicates that this year's convention was one of our most successful events yet, and we thank you for your contribution to this success."* **Larry Goodhope**, Executive Director Alberta Association of Municipal Districts and Counties

*"Thank you, Bob, it is always a pleasure to see a true professional at work. You have made the name 'Speaker' stand out as a truism - someone who encourages people to examine their lives and adjust. The personal stories you shared with your audience made such a great impression on everyone. The comments indicated you hit people right where it is important - in their hearts. Each of those in your audience took away a new feeling of personal success and encouragement."* **Sherry Knight**, Dimension Eleven Human Resources and Communications

*"Bob is one of those rare individuals who knows how to tackle obstacles in life to reach his dreams. He takes each as a learning experience and stretches for more. His compassion and genuine interest in others make him an exceptional coach."* **Cindy Kindret**, former Training Manager, Silk FM Radio

*"Without doubt, I have gained immeasurable self-assurance. Bob, your patience and your encouragement has been much appreciated. I strongly recommend your course to anyone looking for self-improvement and professional development."* **Jeannie Mura**, Human Resources Chevron Canada

*"I am pleased to recommend Bob 'Idea Man' Hooey to any organization looking for a charismatic, confident speaker and seminar leader. I have seen Bob in action on several occasions, and he is ALWAYS on! Bob can grab his audience's attention and keep it. Quite simply, if Bob is involved - your program or seminar is guaranteed to succeed."* **Maurice Laving**, Coordinator Training and Development, London Drugs

*"I have found Bob's attention to detail and his ability to fine tune his seminars to match the time frame and needs of the audience to be a valuable asset to our educational Program."* **Patsy Schell**, Executive Director Surrey Chamber of Commerce

*"Great seeing you in Cancun and congratulations on a job well done. The seminar was a great success! Your humorous and conversational style was a tremendous asset. It is my sincere hope that we can be associated again at future seminars."* **Donald MacPherson**, Attorney At Law, Phoenix, Arizona

*"What a great conference. It was a great pleasure meeting with you at the Ritz Carlton, Cancun and I shall look forward to hopefully welcoming you and your family in Dublin, Ireland someday."* **A. Paul Ryan**, Petronva Corporation, Dublin, Ireland

*"Congratulations on the Spirit of CAPS Award. You have worked long and hard on behalf of CAPS ...helped many speakers including me and richly deserve this award. Well done my friend."* **Peter Legge**, CSP, Hof, CPAE

*"On very short notice Bob cleared his schedule and graciously presented at our meeting when the original Speaker was unable to attend.* **Last week Bob set the tone for our two-day leadership meeting and gave us all a motivational lift.** *His compassion and true interest in people was clearly evident, making him very credible. He shared some great stories, has a wealth of experience and knowledge and it was a pleasure listening to him. His down-to-Earth style makes it easier to retain the information presented. He also followed up with additional info and handouts, cementing his message of building bridges, not walls. Fantastic job, Bob, and thanks again!"* **Barbara Afra Beler**, MBA, Senior Specialist Commercial Community, Alberta North, **BMO Bank of Montreal**

*"I have been so excited working with Bob Hooey, as he has given inspiration and motivation to our leadership team members. Both at the Brick Warehouse – Alberta and here at Art Van Furniture – Michigan; with his years of experience in working with business executives and his humorous and delightful packaging of his material, he makes learning with Bob a real joy. But most importantly, anyone who encounters his material is the better for it."*

**Kim Yost**, CEO Art Van Furniture, former CEO The Brick

- **Motivate your teams**, your employees, and your leaders to 'productively' grow and 'profitably' succeed!
- **Protect your conference investment** - leverage your training dollars.
- **Enhance your professional career** and sell more products and services.
- **Equip and motivate your leaders** and their teams to grow and succeed, 'even' in tough times!
- **Leverage your time** to enhance your skills, equip your teams, and better serve your clients.
- **Leverage your leadership** and investment of time to leave a significant legacy!

**Call today** to engage best-selling author, award winning, inspirational leadership keynote speaker, leaders' success coach, and employee development trainer, Bob 'Idea Man' Hooey and his innovative, audience based, results-focused, **Ideas At Work!** for your next company, convention, leadership, staff, training, or association event. You'll be glad you did!

**Call 1-780-736-0009** to connect with Bob 'Idea Man' Hooey today!

Learn more about Bob at: **www.ideaman.net** or **www.BobHooey.training.**

## Harness the power of 'gratitude.'

When you are reminded of the 'positive' things – the things that are going right in your life, you get a boost of energy and it helps you remain focused on working more productively. I have a list of people and accomplishments I am grateful for in my life and career. I have a 'warm fuzzy' file on my laptop for kudos and acknowledgements from people. When I need them, I simply open it and read! I get inspired again!

# Thanks for reading 'Prepare Yourself to WIN!'
## *Idea-rich success secrets*

Each time I prepare to step on the stage; each time I sit down to write, or in this case to re-write, I am challenged to ensure I deliver something that will be of **use-it-now value** to my reader.

- I ask myself, "If I was reading this, what would I be looking for?"
- As well as "Why is this relevant to me, today?"

**These two questions help to keep me focused** and help me to remain clear on my objectives. They help to remind me to dig into my experiences, stories, examples, and research to provide solid information that will be of benefit and help my readers, when they apply it, succeed. That can be an exciting challenge!

I trust I have done that for you in this updated **'Prepare Yourself to WIN!'** This is my attempt to capture some of the lessons learned *first-hand* serving on various teams and in leadership roles and to share them with you. We need more leaders, now, more than ever. The world is crying out for more compassionate and courageous leaders. I hope you will step up and step into your role as a more effective and influential leader.

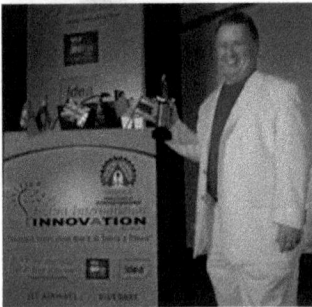

I'd love to hear from you and read your success stories. If you would be so kind, please drop me a quick email at: **bob@ideaman.net**

**Bob 'Idea Man' Hooey**
**2011 Spirit of CAPS recipient**
www.ideaman.net
www.BobHooey.training
www.HaveMouthWillTravel.com
www.SuccessPublications.ca

*Bob in Mumbai, India*